S0-BYN-107

Main to Mudd

An Informal History of Vassar College Buildings

Elizabeth A. Daniels

Photographs by Ben Rayfield and Dixie Sheridan

Vassar College
Poughkeepsie, New York
1987

Main to Mudd was published for the 125th anniversary of Vassar College and funded by the 125th Committee.

Copyright © 1987 by Vassar College
Library of Congress Catalogue
Card Number: 87-50023
ISBN Number: 0-916663-01-9

Production notes. The text was set in Novarese Book, the titles in Novarese Medium Italic, by Bauer Typography, Beacon, NY. Printing—on Warren's Lustro Dull text and cover—and binding by Eastern Press, New Haven, CT. Photographs developed and printed by Charles Porter, published in black and grey duotone, 200-line screen. Design by Ben Rayfield and Dixie Sheridan.

Cover: *Left*, the south tower of Main, Vassar's first building, completed in 1865 and designed by James Renwick, Jr., now a National Historic Landmark. *Right*, the center tower of the Seeley G. Mudd Chemistry building, completed in 1984 and designed by Perry, Dean, Rogers & Partners, Boston. *Photos by Dixie Sheridan.*

Contents

Introduction

Elizabeth A. Daniels' *Main to Mudd* is Vassar's first comprehensive account of the plans, construction, and subsequent fates of Vassar's major buildings. It is a splendid account. How fitting for Vassar's 125th year that Elizabeth Daniels shares with us a portion of her vast knowledge of the college's history!

The narratives of these buildings remind us how we have grown in size and complexity. In Matthew Vassar's day, the entire college, save the Observatory, was contained within the walls of Main. Our campus today speaks to the balance between tradition and progress which has always been basic to Vassar. Each generation designed buildings of architectural distinction and period character. The eclectic styles nevertheless work as a remarkably harmonious whole, a specimen landscape of the architecture of the past 125 years. Vassar's buildings are thus emblematic of our character and educational philosophy: individualistic, bold in aims, and firm of foundations.

Vassar is grateful to Elizabeth Daniels for her long-standing commitment to Vassar. Her scholarly attention to Vassar's past increases our understanding of the importance of preserving our magnificent buildings and our beautiful campus landscape. We must continue to adhere to our traditions and to Matthew Vassar's original vision of excellence.

Frances Daly Fergusson
President, Vassar College
Chair, 125th Committee

Preface

From the beginning Vassar College buildings provided an environment where women could pursue the same quality of education that their brothers and future husbands received at Yale and Harvard. This selective study will show how imaginatively some of these buildings were designed, often initially by the same faculty members who drew up the courses to be taught inside their portals. In the last 125 years, the college has expanded in various directions from the nucleus of Main, the Observatory, and the Calisthenium (Avery). Almost all of the older academic buildings that were used to their limits for several generations of students have been recycled for use by other disciplines and more students.

When Vassar College's first buildings were proposed, there were few collegiate models to follow. Matthew Vassar, however, told his trustees that he had definite ideas for his new campus and its buildings. He wanted "a place that would provide ample apartments for public instruction, and at the same time [afford] the inmates the safety, quiet, privacy, and purity of the family." Before locating and choosing the site of the old Dutchess County racetrack for his original 200-acre campus, Vassar, together with his nephew Matthew Vassar, Jr., and his secretary, Cyrus Swan, tramped over, considered, and rejected many a prospective piece of property. Imagining how passengers on the dayboats might see future college buildings, they explored the bluffs of the Hudson River, and also the flatter acreage two miles inland, where there would be less exposure to the public and ample opportunity for students and faculty to enjoy the benefits of nature's bounties.

The college's first buildings went up during the years of the Civil War. Their Poughkeepsie builder went bankrupt and materials were often delayed in delivery; still the buildings rose with remarkable dispatch, and two of them were ready on schedule for the opening in September 1865. The third, the Calisthenium, was ready in 1866. Vassar would drive out from his country villa, Springside, in the summertime, or from his downtown Vassar Street residence, in other seasons, and offer loving daily supervision.

Through the years the interior spaces of Vassar's buildings have been functionally designed in part by faculty members, sometimes to include laboratories or their equivalents. With so much faculty involvement, the buildings have tended, especially at first, to be individual statements about how subjects ought to be taught or how academic life in a given building should be conducted. This was true, to cite two examples, of Sanders Chemistry (now called Sanders Classroom), designed by chemistry professor Charles Moulton, and Belle Skinner Hall of Music, internally designed by George Sherman Dickinson.

The election of James Monroe Taylor to the presidency of the college in 1886 was a watershed in the college's affairs. In the eight years between President Raymond's death in 1878 and Taylor's arrival, the college under Samuel Caldwell went through some hard times, precipitated most notably by the loss of students to the new competition of Wellesley and Smith, each of which opened in 1875. But by the time of the 25th anniversary in 1890, Taylor had reversed the admission losses, and a significant renaissance was under way. New departments were created, older departments were enlarged, and the faculty was accordingly increased. There were new possibilities for change in these turn-of-the-century years. The suffrage movement began to make its mark. And many more women were thinking of college, as both social work and teaching became appealing vocations.

Through this period buildings slowly spread away from Main to form new centers for campus activity. Still, the campus stayed protected by its hedges and beautiful trees, and continued to enjoy the pleasures and immunities of its cloistered environment. But as the years went on, the college community increased, and students sought and won new freedoms, including the freedom to develop and enforce their own rules and regulations. The "lady principal," as she was called, who presided over the non-academic life of the students from 1865 to 1913, was no more to be seen after Taylor withdrew. The young, progressive Henry Noble MacCracken, a declared suffragist, arrived from Smith College in 1914.

By 1925 MacCracken had reorganized the administration, expanded the curriculum, and produced an exemplary governance that defined the responsibilities of faculty, students, and trustees. He was an experimenter and innovator, and introduced euthenics into the course of study, a discipline that had received some popularity after World War I (although it remained anathema to quite a few Vassar educators). Blodgett, Kendrick, Cushing, and Wimpfheimer Nursery School were all results of the new interest in euthenics; and, along with Sanders Physics and Belle Skinner Hall of Music, they were suddenly all in the works or in planning stages.

During the MacCracken era, quality of education and quality of building were intimately related in the minds of Vassar's builders and planners. Blodgett was specifically laid out for the discipline of euthenics. Kendrick respected the teachers' needs for a residence with privacy for research and preparation, and at the same time provided common rooms for conviviality and serious interchange. Kenyon offered an individualized approach to athletics in order to help students enjoy physical skills and training. Rockefeller Hall, the library, and Taylor underwent renovation to cater

to the growing number of students and the expansion of the curriculum.

The next group of buildings came in the fifties during the presidency of Sarah Gibson Blanding (1946-1964). They included Marcel Breuer's Ferry House (cooperative) in 1951, followed by Eero Saarinen's Noyes in 1958, and Schweikher and Elting's Chicago Hall in 1959.

During the sixties the prospective bride rejected the suitor, and Vassar and Yale, who had been unofficially connected for decades, decided to go their own ways. In the words of former president Alan Simpson (1964-1977), the women's college would remain in its "historic home" and, like Yale, become coeducational. Once again, Vassar was in a pioneering phase. This time the problem was not creating and implementing a curriculum, but adapting a college plant with facilities for 1,600 women to the much more varied needs of an enlarged and coeducational student body. By 1972 the Town Houses and Terrace Apartments were in place. In 1973 Students' Building was remodeled into the All College Dining Center (ACDC). The following year the College Center was creatively designed to make use of the original walls and structure of Main. Olmsted Hall was then built in order to improve the facilities for the biological sciences. And most recently the Seeley G. Mudd Chemistry Building has given vital support to the chemistry program.

In its anniversary year a coeducational Vassar is still "in beauty dwelling." A facilities planning corporation has systematically rehabilitated a number of buildings and many a structure has had the equivalent of a complete physical. The buildings evoked in this study are but a small proportion of the over 185 structures that make up the Vassar campus. But even in these brief glimpses one cannot help but appreciate the resourcefulness and ingenuity that have gone into the magnificent educational enterprise on the Hudson.

Sources

The background materials used in the preparation of this book have been drawn from disparate sources on the Vassar campus. In the Vassar library, particularly in Special Collections, there are files on some of the buildings and various other records, presidential papers, minutes of meetings, press releases, clippings from newspapers, annual reports, and correspondence. In some cases departments documented the conception, design, and execution of buildings at the time they were built. In others, material was not so obvious or readily available. The records of the buildings department (now Facilities Operations) and especially the assistance of the individuals currently in that office have been invaluable to the research. Because I wanted to produce a readable book, I have omitted lengthy documentation whenever possible. Unless otherwise cited, all sources can be found in Special Collections.

My collaborators from the Press and Information Office are Dixie M. Sheridan, press secretary at Vassar, and Ben Rayfield, publications manager, who served as co-designers and photographers. In one case only do we reproduce a picture from the college's photographic files, that of Vassar Brothers Laboratory, which was torn down in 1938.

I am grateful to Carol Freedman '85 and Geraldine Herron, writer/editor in Press and Information, who were copy editors for this publication; to Maryann Bruno, assistant press secretary, Rebecca Diamond, publications assistant, Allegra Knight, secretary, and Susan Kowalski, administrative assistant, for all their help; as well as to Judith A. Lewittes, executive director of development, for her encouragement. I have been helped by Lisa Browar, curator of rare books and manuscripts; Nancy MacKechnie, assistant curator of rare books and manuscripts; Melissa O'Donnell, administrative secretary, Special Collections; and by several oldtimers and newcomers on the faculty and staff, especially Margaret Wright, professor emeritus of biology; Ruth Timm, professor emeritus of physical education; Curt Beck, professor of chemistry; and Otis Waterman, engineer, Facilities Operations, along with Stephen Saulis, director, Facilities Operations..

Elizabeth A. Daniels '41
Professor Emeritus of English
College Historian

11

Main Building

It seems like a dream, the sudden transmutation of this great lumbering pile of brick and mortar, which hung on my spirit like a mountainous millstone, into a place of light and life.
—President John Raymond's letter to his wife, a few days after the first students arrived at Vassar, September 23, 1865

Main Building or "The College," as it was originally called, was erected between 1861 and 1865. It was Matthew Vassar's ideal of a perfect environment for educating young women.

In 1845 Vassar made a grand tour of Europe. In London, he saw Guy's Hospital, named after Sir Thomas Guy whom he believed to be an ancestor. It was during this trip, Vassar recorded in his diary, that he first dreamed of founding an institution that would perpetuate the Vassar name and use the fortune he had accumulated in the brewery business and other enterprises to benefit society. While in France, he was extremely impressed with the architecture of the Tuileries and the Hôtel de Ville. In fact Vassar's notation, penciled later at the top of a colored lithograph of the Tuileries, says: "Similar to Vassar College."

For ten years after his European trip, Vassar thought about how to execute his dream. He received much conflicting advice from friends, relatives, and outsiders, who had heard about his vision. Lydia Booth, for example, his niece who ran the Cottage Hill seminary for girls in Poughkeepsie, encouraged her Uncle Matt to consider the need for women's education. This need was further emphasized by Milo P. Jewett, a clergyman who purchased and presided over Lydia Booth's school after her death and later became Vassar's first president. By 1855 Vassar was determined to go ahead with a women's college. In fact he was so committed at the time that he employed Thomas Tefft, a young architect from

Boston, to draw up preliminary plans for the college's monumental building. Tefft, however, died four years later in Italy, and so Vassar turned to the prominent New York architect James Renwick, Jr., designer of the Smithsonian. Renwick drew up new plans for the building and supervised its construction and landscaping. The structure was built by William Harloe, a Poughkeepsie contractor who proposed to do the job for $178,200. On a spring day in 1861, Matthew Vassar turned over a spadeful of soil on the northeast corner of the chosen site.

Renwick's design for Main Building was an adaptation of the Second Empire style then in vogue. The building was designed to provide accommodations for both academic and residential life. The central pavilion of the building provided living quarters for the president and lady principal, and most of the classrooms and common rooms. The end pavilions housed the male professors and their families. The connecting transverse links housed students in four-room suites that originally contained no closet space. And wide corridors (conceived by Vassar himself) enabled students to exercise indoors when the weather was bad.

A boiler and gashouse were built 400 feet behind Main Building in order to furnish it with steam heat and gas lighting (which was replaced by electricity when the campus energy system was renovated in 1912). And according to Keene Richards, a twentieth century general manager of the college, it appears that Vassar was the first institution in the world to be heated from a plant installed in a separate building.[1] Matthew Vassar himself, as his letters reveal, was passionately involved in getting this steam heating plant to function. His old-fashioned arrangement, now supplemented by modern controls, remains the basis for much of the system today.

Sheridan

12

Main in the summer of 1986. The spade used 125 years ago by Matthew Vassar for ground-breaking was used again in 1982 by then President Virginia B. Smith to begin the Seeley G. Mudd Chemistry Building.

Technical innovations in 1861 included sliding iron doors for fire protection, 20 miles of pipe to distribute spring water, and the latest in sewage disposal.

Sheridan

The words "Vassar Female College" were originally engraved above the building's entrance, over the graceful double staircase. In February 1867, an act of the New York State legislature removed the word "Female" from the name of the college. The act's passage had originally been requested by the trustees. And so it wasn't long before they also voted to take down the central slab, engraved with the word "Female." Sarah Josepha Hale, editor of *Godey's Lady's Book*, had won her one-person campaign against the dreaded word, which she considered vulgar, offensive, and Darwinian.

Planning for the academic use of Main Building was a challenge. The teachers had never taught advanced courses to women; and women, for the most part, had never been college students. In the beginning, much progressed through trial and error. During the first thirty-one years, until Rockefeller Hall was built in 1896, Main was the primary place in which Vassar education evolved. Initially the building met needs for space quite well, but with time, pressure grew for bigger and better academic space.

In 1872 James S. Post designed an extension that was added to the dining room and kitchen at the rear of the building. And even more significantly, the Frederick Ferris Thompson Annex was appended to the front of the building in 1893. Francis R. Allen, who had designed the Thompson house on the estate "Sonnenberg" in Canandaigua, N.Y., was the architect for the annex. The addition, affectionately referred to as "Uncle Fred's Nose," included a marbled porte-cochère or "Soap Palace" that served as a remodeled entrance to the building. The annex solved the overcrowding problem that had developed in the fourth floor library. (The library had moved from the third to the fourth floor after the art gallery had moved to the remodeled riding academy in 1875.) But the outside turning stairs were destroyed when the annex was built in 1893 and have never been restored.

On February 12, 1918, a fire originating in the kitchen destroyed a large part of the rear wing of the building, with damage estimated at $165,000. As part of the reconstruction, a two-storied dining room was built, designed by architects Allen and Collens. The dining room, endowed by the class of 1880, was called "Underwood Hall," in memory of one of their classmates, Jennie Cushing Underwood.

The building was not altered in any significant way again until 1937, when a section of the ground floor was redesigned to accommodate the Vassar Cooperative Bookshop. At the same time more single room units were provided for students.

In 1959, during Sarah Gibson Blanding's presidency, funds were given by Mr. and Mrs. John D. Rockefeller, 3rd (Blanchette Hooker Rockefeller '31) to restore Main's original facade. (Many people had considered "Uncle Fred's Nose" an aesthetic blight.) That winter the whole college community gawked as a wrecking ball systematically lunged at the nose. Goldstone and Dearborn were the architects for the restoration, and the Campbell Company of Poughkeepsie presided over the demolition.

The College Center, designed by Jean Paul Carlhian of the Boston firm of Shepley, Bulfinch, Richardson, and Abbott, was added to Main in 1977 and won the American Institute of Architects' Honor Award that year.

Main Building has now repossessed some of the functions that were relegated to the outlying dormitories after 1893 and to the Students' Building (now All College Dining Center) after 1914. It is once again the hub of Vassar College's student activities, although the lady principal and corridor mistresses have departed.

In the summer of 1986 Main Building, already listed on the Federal Register (1974), was honored anew by being chosen as a National Historic Landmark along with the Metropolitan Museum of Art, the Plaza Hotel, and the Empire State Building in New York City.

15

Vassar College Observatory

Designed for the practical use of students.
—Architect Charles Farrar's words to the
trustees on June 30, 1863

The first building to be completed and
furnished, the brick and stone
Observatory, was ready when the college
opened in 1865. By 1867 Maria Mitchell, a
noted professor of astronomy, already
had 17 students in her courses, more than
were studying the subject at Harvard or
Yale. Mitchell's classes had many students
even though the requirements for
entrance into the preliminary junior level
courses involved rigorous preparation in
mathematics, a field in which early Vassar
students were often ill prepared.

In 1862 the Rev. Dr. Rufus Babcock, a
trustee, went to Massachusetts to visit
Maria Mitchell on behalf of the astronomy
department. Mitchell, already renowned
throughout the scientific world along with
Caroline Herschel and Mary Somerville,
was then living in Lynn, Massachusetts,
with her father, William, from whom she
had received her early instruction in
astronomy. She agreed to move with her
father to Poughkeepsie, where she would
continue her work in astronomy at the
prospective Vassar Observatory. An
outspoken realist and feminist, Mitchell
helped the college gain its reputation as a
place where students were pushed to
think for themselves and where theory
met practical observations.

Once Mitchell had accepted the
professorship at Vassar, Milo P. Jewett, the
first president, began to consider
arrangements for the construction of the
Observatory. Charles S. Farrar (who
subsequently became Vassar's first
professor of mathematics, physics, and
chemistry) was consulted in the spring of
1863 to develop the plans.

The structure was to be situated about
800 feet northeast of Main Building. And
in September 1863, grounds superintendent

Dubois was authorized to have the crown
of the hill on the proposed site removed
to procure a proper elevation for the
building.

The Observatory, to face west, was
designed to include an octagonal center
of 26 feet in diameter, surmounted by a
dome, 27-feet 7-inches in diameter. Three
identical protruding wings, 21-by-28-feet,
of two stories each, containing various
functional rooms, extended to the north,
east, and south, providing, on the second
story, in order: a prime vertical room, a
transit room, and a clock and chronograph
room—all named for the sensitive
instruments that were to be used in them.
The basement of the wings, unfinished at
first, was 9 feet high, but the floor of the
octagon (which attained the same height
as the wings) was 4½ feet above the floors
of the wings. Brick, the building material
closest to the English founder's Norfolk
heart, was the primary construction
material; the walls of the octagon were
made with solid brick for stability and the
walls of the wings were hollow. The dome
was built with ribs of pine resting on a
plate of pine and covered with sheet-tin.
Sixteen cast-iron pulleys, 9 inches in
diameter and running on a track of iron,
revolved the ton-and-a-half dome.

Five stone piers, spanning the basement
and the principal floors, were uniformly
disconnected from the walls and floors of
the building so as to be "immovable by
wind or any mechanical force." A granite
shaft rested on the most massive pier to
hold the equatorial, with similar shafts for
the transit and meridian circle of
Onondaga limestone, and for the prime
vertical of white Westchester marble. The
bases of the clock and chronograph were
of Dover marble.[2]

Even before Farrar submitted
preliminary plans to the board, Mitchell's
famous telescope was purchased.
Matthew Vassar, personally interested in

Sixteen cast-iron pulleys, nine inches in diameter and running on a track of iron, revolved the ton-and-a-half dome. A granite shaft held the equatorial, with similar shafts of Onondaga limestone for the transit and meridian circle, and white Westchester marble for the prime vertical. The bases of the clock and chronograph were of Dover marble.

Rayfield

the Observatory, told the trustees in 1863 how this was accomplished: Henry Fitz, the celebrated telescope-maker of New York, had on hand an object-glass $12\frac{3}{8}$ inches in diameter, which could be bought for cash down for $2,000 less than the customary price. Through a third party (so the price wouldn't be jacked up if the college were known as the bidder) "the bargain was closed, the treasurer secured the prize, and the glass [was put] in the safe of the founder." Vassar also told the trustees that their new telescope was exceeded in size "only by the great equatorial at Cambridge University." (He probably meant Harvard.)

Farrar, in planning the building so that the college might have the best of everything, consulted with one Mr. Rutherford of New York and, at Rutherford's suggestion, Professors Loomis of Yale and Orrin Root of Hamilton College. Farrar pointed out to the trustees that all the then existing observatories were for observers only, and that the Vassar laboratory would "take precedence over all others in being designed for the practical use of students."

It was reported to the board in February 1864 that William Harloe, builder of Main, had begun work on the Observatory, that "[a] telegraph line was put up within 1,000 rods of the building, thus affording at small expense an opportunity to connect with the observatories at Washington, Albany, Cambridge, and elsewhere." (The college had the good fortune to have Samuel F. B. Morse as neighbor and trustee.) By June of 1864 the building was finished, and Farrar occupied it until Mitchell arrived. In 1865, she and her father would move into the somewhat unfinished north wing. "Can you do something before my return," she wrote in the summer of 1866 to Cyrus Swan, the college's supervisor, "to make the basement room of the Observatory more presentable?" "Will you, in our absence," she wrote earlier that first year, "have the goodness to look into the Observatory

and see if some arrangements can be made for greater domestic comfort?" The fact was, because scientific arrangements took precedence, domestic provisions had been neglected in the building's initial planning.

Mitchell's favorite astronomical studies, according to her first student and successor Mary Whitney '68, were Jupiter and Saturn. In fact, at a time when there was no foundation money for faculty assistance, Mitchell, at her own expense, printed observations about these planets in the scientific magazine *Silliman's Journal*. She also constructed an apparatus for photographing the sun, and her photographs and recorded observations have been preserved.

Mitchell's reports to the presidents over the years from 1871 to 1886 reveal the caliber of her teaching, and the enthusiasm and ability of her students. For example, she reported that her undergraduates were instructed in their junior year to use instruments; "small telescopes and a transit instrument [were] put into their hands and they [were] allowed to practice with the meridian circle." Seniors could study solar eclipses and predict them by the most rigorous method in their final examinations. During nine evenings in 1871-72, "a series of observations on Jupiter" were open to visitors, Mitchell noted.

In addition to their work at the Observatory, Mitchell's students had the opportunity to go out into the field. One graduate and six former students traveled to observe a total eclipse of the sun in Burlington, Iowa, on August 7, 1869, and their recorded observations were later printed in an official report of the eclipse by Professor J. H. C. Coffin. Mitchell would often ask her classes, "Did you learn that from a book or did you observe it yourself?" In this way, she trained her students in the methods of genuine scientific inquiry.

As time passed, two of Mitchell's most distinguished students followed her as

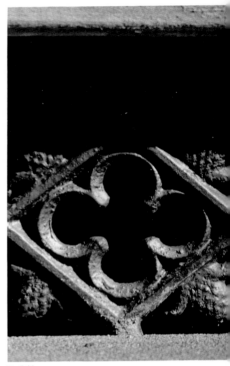

Rayfield

A detail from the staircase. In early 1986, 1,200 Poughkeepsians saw Halley's Comet from Maria Mitchell's old haunt.

Rayfield

"Did you learn that from a book or did you observe it yourself?" Mitchell asked her students.

astronomers: the aforementioned Mary Whitney and Caroline Furness '91, who was, in turn, Mary Whitney's student. When we consider Mitchell's teaching, we can see that women at Vassar, even in the early years, were receiving an education in science as good as, if not better than, what men were being offered at their colleges. (In February 1987 Vera C. Rubin '48 continues the tradition as the President's Distinguished Visitor.)

Alas, the Observatory, which was altered a few times through the years (including the enlargement of living quarters for its early tenants), now serves as a general academic building. Some rooms are currently used as a college resource center, while others are used for the study of Chinese. But in Vassar's game of musical chairs, astronomy students have moved to Sanders Physics, where they now use computers instead of telescopes. And the Observatory can no longer be used for the fine work of astronomy in the space age. City lights and electronic disturbance in recent decades have interfered with observation and measurement, resembling the earlier effects of coal dust. In January and March 1986, however, the Observatory became the site of an astronomical revival, when 1,200 Poughkeepsians turned out to observe the faint manifestations of Halley's Comet. It was almost like the old comet-gazing times.

The dome no longer resounds with the laughter of guests at one of Mitchell's famous dome parties—occasions where, the early students recall, the professor always produced personal rhymes. In fact at her fiftieth reunion in 1924, Annie Howes Barus remembered one of Mitchell's dome party rhymes about Florence Cushing '74:

"Massachusetts claims Miss Cushing Always leading, never pushing."

The Calisthenium, the third building to rise on what in 1866 was a treeless plain, is now Avery, surrounded by trees, ivy, and other buildings.

Sheridan

The Calisthenium and Riding Academy

No building at Vassar has changed functions more than the Calisthenium and Riding Academy. In 1866 the *New York Times* said that it was the most beautiful structure of its kind in the country, second in size only to the gymnasium at West Point. An examination of this kind of building—the college's first gymnasium—also reflects an anti-Victorian theme in Matthew Vassar's educational philosophy. Unlike his contemporaries, he believed that rigorous exercise should play an important role in a healthy woman's life.

The red brick building, with the same color patterns as the Observatory and Main, was designed by J. A. Wood, a Poughkeepsie architect who also designed, among other buildings, Vassar Brothers Institute, erected by Matthew Vassar's nephews, and Vassar Brothers Home for Aged Men, built on the site of Matthew Vassar's city residence. Its original purpose was to provide a place for required systematic exercise and horseback riding. Since 1873, when its original functions as riding academy and stable were abandoned as too costly, the building has been renovated and renamed several times.

An 1863 prospectus of the college stated: "A sound mind in a sound body is received as a first truth among educators. In our plan of education . . . we must include Anatomy. . . Physiology. . . Hygiene, by which we are taught the laws of health and the art of preserving it." Victorian views of women, holding them incapable of being serious students because of physical and mental limitations, presented a serious challenge that had to be met and combated.

Defying this public prejudice, Vassar's first catalogue announced that the college would provide a systematic program of physical culture called "light gymnastics." The program was to be based on the principles of health laid down by Dr. Dio Lewis, whose "Home School of Physical Culture," in Lexington, Massachusetts, provided a radical, innovative, and provocative program for women's health care.

The catalogue stated: "The gymnasium will be furnished with every variety of apparatus required to make it attractive and useful . . . ." Vassar's program required that exercise be daily, vigorous, and systematic. Every day each Vassar student would be required to do "new gymnastics" for two to four half-hour periods. For pupils with physical "deficiencies," there would be specialized Swedish exercises. And, as one might expect, this regimen meant a change in lifestyle: daily requirements of plain, nutritious food, fixed hours for rising and retiring, warm and cold baths, regular morning and evening walks, and "physiological dress" for exercise.

During 1865 the Calisthenium was still under construction. So the physical education instructor, Elizabeth M. Powell, conducted her classes in Main Building's wide corridors, specifically designed so that during bad weather students and professors alike could walk briskly back and forth from one end of the building to the other. Each round trip would yield approximately one-fifth of a mile's exercise.

In time for the second academic year, the athletics building was completed. It included a calisthenics hall with equipment, a riding arena and stalls for horses, a bowling alley, music practice rooms, and a concert hall and stage. The "calisthenics hall" section of the building (on its north side) was 30-by-80-feet and completely supplied with the Lewis gymnastic equipment. The central portion of the building housed the riding arena (60-feet wide by 120-feet long by 46-feet high), which had good ventilation. There was a hay loft in the back of the building.

two stories high. And in the basement: stalls for twenty-three horses, a carriage room, carpenters' and joiners' shops, rooms for other college employees and living quarters for the family of Baron Leopold von Seldeneck, the German riding teacher who had been a Civil War cavalry master.

By 1873 the horses in the riding academy were costing too much. This was the opinion of Cyrus Swan, the college's first business manager and Matthew Vassar's former private secretary and lawyer, who kept meticulous records of purchases. Even though the baron took in supplementary pupils from Poughkeepsie girls academies, the effort failed financially. The building was renamed the Museum in 1875 after it was overhauled at a cost of $27,000—to the protest, however, of the *Miscellany*, which objected by writing: "The glory of Vassar is departed. False economy. Would the art gallery [in Main] be abolished if it did not pay?"

The hayloft portion of the building was transformed into music rooms. (In fact, since 1932 these cubicle rooms have been occupied by English and drama department faculty, one of whom smelled hay in the back of her office when she came in first thing in the morning.) The old riding arena had a skylight placed above it and became the new quarters for the art gallery, which moved over from Main Building's fourth floor. The gymnasium, along with the basement bowling alley, remained in service. Scientific cabinets from Main's ground floor were moved to the front of the renovated academy where an enlarged museum of natural history, to be used for pedagogical purposes, was created. The dramatic hall, called "Society Hall," was moved from the first floor to the second. And a science lecture room was created on the first floor, along with a laboratory and room for the music professor.

Louisa May Alcott, coming to the February 1875 dedication of the renovated building, was the talk of the campus. For weeks after her visit, a group of students called each other by names from *Little Men* and *Little Women* and playfully assumed their literary identities as they went about their activities.[3]

After calisthenics was moved to another building in 1890, the former gymnasium was used as a hall of casts. It included plaster casts of Ghiberti's bronze doors, then recent acquisitions, and casts of famous Greek and Roman statues. In 1915 painting classes and the art gallery were moved from the Museum to the newly built Taylor Hall. But when the great fire of 1918 destroyed Main's rear wing, the Museum became the new location for the assembly room and was accordingly renamed Assembly Hall. From that time on, the Assembly Hall stage was the scene of lectures and various dramatic activities, culminating in the Experimental Theater.

The building was officially renamed Avery Hall in 1931 in honor of Alida C. Avery, the first resident physician and professor of hygiene and physiology (1865-1874). In 1932 music classes were moved from Avery to the newly built Belle Skinner Hall of Music. At the same time, the classics and English departments moved to Avery from Rockefeller Hall, thus ending years of agitation by the English department for more office and conference space. (It was reported by Laura Wylie '77, chairperson of the English department in the late 1890s, that English instructors were forced to rent student sitting rooms in Main for their conferences.) More recently still, there have been minor internal rearrangements in Avery: the drama department has long since separated from the English department, and the remaining museum collections have been relocated. Future plans call for a new home for the English department in Sanders Classroom (formerly Sanders Chemistry) and another renovation of Avery for drama and other departments.

Sheridan

Avery's stable facade masked the ever-changing interior space which has been hayloft, joiner shop, bowling alley, hall of casts, home for Baron Von Seldeneck, and host to Louisa May Alcott.

23

Vassar Brothers Laboratory

And up there two miles from the city, hanging onto civilization by the skirts as it were, like a baby to its mother's gown. It is a sort of poem, in the vast volume of prose one goes through to get to it.
—Emily Faithfull, April 27, 1883, in the *New York Star*

On April 15, 1880, the *Albany Argus* called Vassar Brothers Laboratory "one of the most convenient, roomy, and perfectly equipped chemistry laboratories in America." Forty-five by sixty-five feet, with three stories of brick and slate, this building was even "more striking than Main Building," which stood about 500 feet away. The laboratory was given to the college by Matthew Vassar's two trustee nephews, Matthew Vassar, Jr., and John Guy Vassar. It was conceived and overseen by LeRoy C. Cooley, professor of chemistry. The architectural adviser to the project was Professor Benjamin Silliman, Jr., whose father had been the first professor of chemistry at Yale University and the Sheffield Scientific School. Silliman, Jr., had been his father's assistant before striking out on his own as an architect and as the first petroleum geologist in the United States.

Vassar Brothers Laboratory was still standing when New England Building was built in 1901, Sanders Hall of Chemistry in 1909, and Sanders Hall of Physics in 1925. The laboratory was slated to be torn down in 1925, but its psychologist tenants successfully resisted the mandatory move. With their associates in economics, they stayed in Vassar Brothers Laboratory until 1938 when the building was deemed unfit for use. These faculty members, many of whom had no use for the interdisciplinary subject of euthenics, finally moved under protest to Blodgett, which housed that department.

No other structure on the campus has ever moved so quickly from the dreams of the desiring faculty to bricks and mortar.

On June 24, 1879, President Samuel Caldwell made it known to the trustees that Professor Cooley thought that new quarters for the teaching of chemistry and physics were urgently needed. On April 16, 1880, less than a year later, the new laboratory was opened "with appropriate services."

From the first days of the college, chemistry had been taught along with physics in Room C on the first floor of Main Building, where the director of residence is currently housed. Vassar followed the method of teaching physical science through experimentation that had been popularized by Professor Benjamin Silliman, Sr., at Yale in 1806. In fact from that date on, the developments in Silliman's classrooms and subsequently in his laboratories set the pace for the teaching of chemistry, mineralogy, and geology in the United States. That the chemistry and physics classes initiated at Vassar were based on Silliman's model was very much in keeping with Matthew Vassar's desire to offer women the same quality of education in the sciences that men received.

Those first years, however, must have been somewhat difficult for the students. In 1879, Caldwell pointed out to the trustees that the facilities were not large enough for the 176 students in the department of physics and chemistry. Cooley felt that the health of the science professors and students was at stake: there was no escape from impure air and noxious gases on Main's first floor. Both Caldwell and Cooley recognized that a new and separate building was absolutely required. Their decision was further influenced by the fact that a recent explosion in the chemistry lab at Lafayette College had incurred $300,000 worth of property damages.

Vassar's first chemistry building was the first separate chemistry laboratory in a college for women. It was built in less than a year, 1879-80, for $10,000. One hundred years later, building Mudd chemistry laboratory on that site cost $7.2 million.

Caldwell was concerned that without enough laboratory space Vassar might not be able to maintain its stature in the world of scientific education. He observed that instruments valued at thousands of dollars were crowded into too small a space. Caldwell believed that lack of light was one of the worst problems. During two-thirds of the college year, there was no direct sunlight in Room C, and occasionally it was so dark that the gas had to be lit.

Before the fall of 1879, the building was under way. Matthew Vassar, Jr., himself solicited the bids from local builders, plumbers, and outfitters, and no time was lost in starting. The building was built and supplied with ample equipment for $10,000. As later reported by Taylor, one interesting episode occurred at the beginning of the construction. Matthew Vassar, Jr., for reasons of his own, wanted the laboratory to be placed exactly where it was eventually built. Cooley, however, wanted it set to the true meridian, while the grounds superintendent insisted it should "square" with Main. Cooley moved the stakes secretly after they had been initially placed in accordance with Vassar's wishes. The latter discovered Cooley's insubordination and personally replaced them, declaring that anything else would have "queered" the south end of the campus. (Students of the college after 1938 could tell where the building had been located because the original doorstep stone was preserved as a bench exactly where the old doorstep had been set.)

The architectural sketch for Vassar Brothers Laboratory shows that the ground floor was to be designated for physics: with a room for "apparatus," a lecture room, space for stores and preparation of materials, and an office for the professor. On the second floor would be a large chemistry laboratory for students, a private one for the professor, and a room for scales and balances.

At the opening ceremonies, Cooley pointed out: "For the main chemical laboratory good light is secured by its numerous windows looking to the east, the south and the west. Good air is insured by means of flues which furnish ventilation from the ceiling and from the floor, and also by means of . . . *ventilating chambers*, easy of access from all parts of the room, providing a quick exit for offensive fumes. Sixty-two working tables are arranged in three groups. Each table is supplied with a set of reagent and specimen bottles; with gas, water, sink and filter pump. In two of the groups, each table is provided with a double set of drawers and cupboards so that it can accommodate two students working at different periods."

Freestanding laboratory work had been developed only at places like the Sheffield Scientific School and the Massachusetts and Stevens Institutes of Technology. So Cooley reminded his audience that the sort of facilities that Vassar Brothers Laboratory provided was virtually unknown as an adjunct to regular courses in the liberal arts. "But," he emphasized, "underneath these technical and university courses there lies the academic course in Arts for general culture, and in this department of our colleges and universities the facilities for the practical study of chemistry and physics are very limited and in most cases altogether unknown."

Cooley pleaded eloquently for courses in chemistry and physics in this new facility that were equally made up of lecture, library, and laboratory time. In making his case, he remarked: "The experimental study of chemistry is a slow method. A few years have been sufficient to demonstrate [the Vassar student's] success in the college course; few more will be needed to enable woman to demonstrate her ability to pursue the higher courses to the university and out into practical life."

The Alumnae Gymnasium

Selecting a site for the alumnae gym to the north and east of Main signaled a willingness to expand the campus beyond the shadow of Main.

Sheridan

27

Here's to the new gym-na-sium
Built by the enterprising alum
Did we assist them?
Well, I guess so-some
Here's to the new gym-na-sium.
—1889 Student Yell

In 1883 the Boston alumnae, led by Florence Cushing, announced that Vassar's physical education program (the first of its kind in the country) was falling behind those in the newly opened sister colleges, Smith and Wellesley. Although the Calisthenium had been state-of-the-art in 1866, it was outmoded by 1883. So it wasn't long before the Boston and New York clubs were trying to raise the $20,000 they thought a new athletics building would cost. And by early 1889, a trustee-alumnae committee had selected a site to the north and east of Main.

The chosen location satisfied most everyone's requirements. According to President Taylor in 1889, it was near enough to the power plant, which would heat the new gymnasium. It was situated so that "the view from the Observatory should not be trespassed upon." And it was fairly close, but not too close, to Main. In short, it was near enough so as to be reached conveniently, and "yet so far away that carelessness as to warmth of clothing would not be encouraged."

Creating the proper internal plan for the new athletics building was a complicated task. The Students' Association wanted more than the school could afford: a swimming bath, a tennis court, a bowling alley, and space for calisthenics and supervised exercise. By June 7, 1887, the Alumnae Association had already raised between $18,000 and $20,000. (The money came in from a variety of sources. The class of '89 gave $148, the class of '90, $263. Philaletheis, the dramatic society, which hoped also to have space in the building, gave $41. Assorted individuals gave $50 apiece. Mary Morris Pratt '80, treasurer of the committee and wife of a trustee who gave many other

endowments to the college, doubled the sum for a total of $1,004 early in 1887. John Guy Vassar and Mary Thaw Thompson '87 pledged $6,000.) On September 4, 1887, all $20,000 was placed in the hands of the committee.

William M. Tubby, who had designed the Pratt Gymnasium at Amherst, as well as the Trades School at Pratt Institute, was hired to draw up architectural plans. Because builders in Poughkeepsie estimated that expenses would run between $39,997 and $50,000, the trustees appointed a subcommittee to try to modify Tubby's plans. During the summer of 1888 they obtained estimates from builders in Brooklyn, Albany, Troy, Rondout, and Kingston. Still, the lowest estimate was too high—$32,000.

In October the original architectural scheme was totally abandoned. The new building would only contain an exercise hall and dressing rooms. The $20,000 already in pocket, would have to remain the limit, and no more money was to be solicited. On February 4, 1889, however, Tubby was permitted to present another plan; brick was substituted for stone, the size of the main exercise hall was reduced, and a visitors' gallery and running track (which was to have been suspended from the roof) were omitted. The planned building, however, included many amenities: 40 dressing rooms, 25 "needle baths" opening into dressing rooms, 3 water closets, 3 stationary washbowls, and a swimming bath, 47-by-27-feet (the largest in any school or college in the country). The physical education director's room was to be on the second floor in the front southwest tower. And the hall above the dressing rooms (47-by-100-feet) was to be used for tennis and Philaletheis plays. (In fact the three annual plays—called Hall Plays—that became a tradition years later were named after the theatrical productions that used to be performed in the old Alumnae Gymnasium hall.)

One Mr. Otis of Kingston was hired as builder. The contract was signed. Ground

A running track was to have been suspended from the roof of the gymnasium. True to the original design, Philaletheis again uses the building for its productions, most recently *Torch Song Trilogy.*

Sheridan

29

was broken on March 26, 1889. And by October the building was ostensibly finished. Its swimming bath with marble facing was donated by the ever-benevolent Frederick Ferris Thompson, known as the "good times trustee." Immediately, however, it was discovered that the original stairway was not safe enough; so a second stairway was installed with another exit from the building. In 1890 a visiting committee of trustees identified some other problems which were corrected, such as inadequate fire escapes. The college also had to procure water for the swimming bath by means of a 150-foot-deep artesian well. But by June 11, 1890, the alumnae were finally ready to make a formal presentation of the building to the trustees.

Because the college was becoming overcrowded, the use of the building had already shifted by September 1892. The trustees voted to make the second story of the gymnasium an assembly hall for day students and those resident students who had been relegated to the Windsor Hotel in Poughkeepsie. Shockingly, by 1897 the building was too small to meet the college's athletic needs. Room A on the first floor of Main (where the chemistry lecture room had been) was consequently fitted up as a temporary auxiliary gym. In 1901 a subcommittee was already looking into ways to enlarge the gym; and by June 12, 1905, fifteen years after the building was inaugurated, $25,000 was allotted by the trustees to enlarge it. William Downing was to be the new architect.

The building was remodeled two more times. The first group of changes occurred in 1933 when doctors offices and a nurses suite were added. The building was then renamed Ely in honor of Achsah M. Ely '68, professor of mathematics from 1887 to 1904, who had spearheaded the original alumnae drive for funds. In this move physical education graduated again to a new building (after a span of forty-five years), and the title Alumnae Gymnasium no longer reflected the building's function.

The second change occurred in 1937. Thomas Hills, professor of geology, together with Keene Richards, general manager, drew up plans to move geology from New England Building to Ely. In addition, applied art students were given more space with four large rooms on the second floor of Ely. Meanwhile the old gym was made into an official faculty gathering place, and the faculty as a body moved its regular meetings over from Rockefeller. The room was dubbed the Aula, after the tradition in European universities.

Thus Vassar's second gymnasium—the two-story brick building in Romanesque style with a circular tower on the southwest corner and a main entrance porch—has seen quite a few changes since its inception in 1883 and completion in 1890. Many of these alterations were responses to the demands of new times. In fact, the prominent vision of the campus changed significantly when Ely was built. Main was no longer the college's absolute center of life; change and expansion were in the air.

After 1890 Taylor stopped accepting special students, regular enrollments were on the increase, the faculty was enlarged and subdivided into new and expanding departments, and pressure to increase academic and extracurricular space intensified. The college began to use more of its land, and the principle of accessibility to Main, which had dominated the campus, was becoming less important as the institution grew more complex and centers of activity shifted.

Strong House and the Quadrangle

Rayfield

By the 1890s, the resident faculty were desperate to get out of Main and students wanted less crowded and less regulated living conditions. The trustees agreed to build Strong, above, a modified Elizabethan building.

31

The problem of the accommodation of students is. . .a pressing one. The building |Main| is practically full; it will never again be possible to require students to room as they did in the early days of the college. . . .Whatever may be the disadvantages of the so-called 'cottage system' it is now in favor, and we must in some way meet the popular want.
—President Taylor to trustees, October 1889

By the 1890s the Vassar campus needed a master plan. Faculty and students alike agitated for less restricted, less regulated, and less crowded living conditions. The idea of living under one protective roof still dominated the thinking of some—especially trustees—which accounted for the decision to keep the library in Main. The college had to respond: the question was, how. People like Frederick Ferris Thompson favored adding to Main, either on the front lawn or on the north side towards the Noyes circle. But the resident faculty wanted desperately to get out of their apartments at either end of Main and into their own houses. The first crack in the old arrangements came when the trustees agreed in 1889 to build two houses across Raymond Avenue for individual male faculty members and their families. (The women would have to wait a while before Williams was built.) Thompson first committed himself to pay for one house, then two. Finally, the trustees agreed that four should be built at once, with the college paying for the other two. Francis Allen was the architect for all of them. Taylor then seized further initiative and recommended a separate student dormitory. The trustees agreed to spend $75,000 for the building. But it wasn't long after Allen finished plans for the dormitory that a shortage of $35,000 was discovered. Taylor sent a telegram to trustee John D. Rockefeller pleading dire need. Rockefeller generously agreed to endow the building, and it was named after his daughter Bessie Rockefeller Strong, a special student (1886-88).

Next was the decision on location.

There were a number of considerations. The recitation rooms, chapel, and library were in Main; the new gymnasium had purposely been located near Main; and the laboratory buildings were south of Main. The new building had to be convenient to all of them.

The site picked for Strong met all the requirements, and the trustees decreed that the building should overlook the gardens of the circle, just as Noyes would later.

The modified Elizabethan brick building provided single rooms for 100 students, which seemed about right—a good number to live in one house so long as the dining room ceilings were kept high enough to afford quiet at mealtime. By 1895 applicants for rooms in Strong exceeded accommodations. So in conjunction with the construction of Rockefeller, Raymond, another Allen-designed dormitory, was built in 1897.

At this point, consultant Frederick Olmsted, according to Taylor, recommended that future buildings at the north end of the campus be arranged in what he described as an "echelon formation."[4] He thought it would be better if the campus could develop a more open sense of space. But Francis Allen and the firm of York and Sawyer, architects of Rockefeller, disagreed and thought that the effect would be "the appearance of two long unbroken rows of buildings on the bias." That is how a quadrangular plan was chosen. "The coal road around the end of the campus was given up, the cedar hedge was eradicated, and," according to Taylor, "the college for the first time since the early days enjoyed a vista of the great north campus."

When it came to planning Lathrop House in 1901 and Davison in 1902, there were no new problems, the style of each building having been preset by the nature of the quadrangle. Lathrop was built with college funds and named after Dr. Edward Lathrop, a charter trustee whose daughter Julia Lathrop '80 was a prominent alumna.

Sheridan

32

The quadrangle in 1986. Trustee John D. Rockefeller agreed to endow Strong, named for his daughter, and later, in 1902, he gave Davison House, named for his mother.

John D. Rockefeller agreed to give Davison House, and it was named for Eliza Davison, his mother.

By 1905 no more than 1,000 students could be registered at Vassar for each new term. Nonetheless, the college needed to increase its dormitory space. So it wasn't long before the decision to build a fifth dormitory was finalized. For a design, the college turned to Lewis Pilcher, professor of art from 1900 to 1911, and later architect for New York State, during which time he designed Sing Sing prison. The plans drawn up by Pilcher were very different from the harmonious dormitory quadrangle and from the style of Rockefeller Hall. His four-story building of brick and stone included two dining rooms, and a nine-story square tower, designed, it was said, to help campus water pressure. The building was U-shaped and generally Tudor in spirit. Built with college funds, it was called "North" until officials concluded in 1915, at the time of the fiftieth anniversary, that no donor was forthcoming. Thereafter it was called Jewett, after Milo P. Jewett, Vassar's first president, who clearly influenced early plans for the college, but who resigned under pressure before the college opened. (Edna St. Vincent Millay was rumored to have threatened to throw herself from Jewett tower, but fortunately she graduated with the class of 1917.)

In 1912 Allen designed Olivia Josselyn House, endowed by Mrs. Russell Sage and named to honor her mother. It is made of brick and trimmed with stone. Strictly speaking, Josselyn is not a quadrangle dormitory, but it was certainly oriented with respect to Jewett. It is largely free of northern rooms and, like Jewett, was built in a U-shape, has battlements, and faces south. (Josselyn was the first *dormitory* on the campus to have showers although, as we have already heard, the earlier-built Alumnae Gym had twenty-five of them.)

33

Emma Hartman Noyes House

Opened in the fall of 1958, Noyes was the last dormitory to be built. It was given by descendants of Emma Hartman Noyes (1880), and designed by Eero Saarinen, husband of Aline Saarinen '35.

"Snugly encased in its polyethylene envelope," as a press release put it, Noyes was built to accommodate 156 students and two house fellows with their families. The four-storied red brick building curves around one-quarter of a grass circle, which, since Vassar and Renwick designed it, has been used for recreation. In the earliest years, riding students rode around the large ring encircling the lawn. As time went on, the green was used for tennis, archery, and many Founder's Day picnics. It was even the scene of a nude-in in the early seventies.

The handsome building was intended to be the first of two identical building units that should have formed a semicircle along the northern side of the circle. As it happened, the college decided to forgo the other part of the semicircle to build the Town Houses and Terrace Apartments instead.

The interior design for the dining room and lounge in Noyes was created by the architect. Toadstool-shaped chairs in the lounge matched the toadstool entrances and reflected the natural surroundings. After the All College Dining Center was built, the kitchen area of Noyes was converted into the West End coffeehouse, which until very recently has provided an alternative to Matthew's Mug and other campus nightspots. The lounge, with its "passion-pit," has occasionally been used as a theater-in-the-round, as it was one particular night during Alan Simpson's administration when William Rothwell, then instructor in drama, directed a reading of A Christian Oratorio: For the Time Being by W. H. Auden, sponsored by the Christian Fellowship.

Rayfield

34

Noyes, the last dormitory to be built on campus, looks out on the grass circle which Matthew Vassar and James Renwick designed for recreation. Today, Frisbee has replaced tennis on the green.

Rockefeller Hall

Fill these empty rooms with light.
—From "Dedicatory Hymn," written by Fanny L. McKinney '98 for the dedication of Rockefeller Hall, November 19, 1898

Rockefeller Hall, the college's first all-purpose academic building, was erected in 1897 in response to a need for more recitation hall space. Designed by York and Sawyer in what has been called a Victorian modified-Elizabethan style, "Rocky" ushered in the systematic development of the quadrangle, dispersing the life of the college somewhat away from Main Building to the north. The new hall, easily accessible with its many entrances, was made from ubiquitous Vassar brick, although it departed from the French mansard style of Main. Like Bessie Strong House (1893) and Eliza Davison House (1902), Rockefeller Hall was endowed by John D. Rockefeller, Vassar benefactor and trustee from 1888 to 1905.

Although the science laboratories and classrooms had been moved to new and remodeled buildings by the turn of the century, Taylor's ambitious plans for development nonetheless called for more space. As president, he immediately began reorganizing the college program. One of his most significant projects was eliminating the preparatory division, which until 1891 had diluted the college's fiscal, academic, and spatial resources.

It was certainly just as difficult to find a building donor in 1895 as it is now. Taylor, then on a seven-month leave of absence, wrote John D. Rockefeller from Rome requesting his support. Upon his return on Founder's Day, Kate Strong Sewall '91, an undergraduate related to Rockefeller by marriage, relayed the message that Rockefeller would give $100,000 for the academic building. (The building, when completed, actually cost $99,998.75.)

According to the original plan, the building was only to be used during the day, to keep students from going out after dark. Indeed, until quite recently, it has not been used much at night except for occasional lectures.

Before Rocky was built, almost all of the courses in the college, except those in science, were taught in Main or, occasionally, in other emergency locations, such as the Windsor Hotel, half way down Main Street in Poughkeepsie. Until the inauguration of Rocky, there was no appropriate place for student-teacher conferences. Faculty members wanting to confer with students out of class had to create their own meeting places. There was no privacy to provide the sense of professionalism that many of the early faculty wanted. When the college was young, many of the classes were lectures. In the Taylor years, however, a new attitude developed towards learning that emphasized the value of individual conferences. In her annual report to the president in 1906, for example, Laura Wylie, chairperson of the English department, pleaded for more office space so that instructors could meet with students without having to rent student sitting rooms.

Rockefeller Hall has been enlarged and renovated several times since 1897. As more buildings were constructed and as the academic program changed, departments moved in and out of Rocky. In 1916, two seminar rooms and ten offices were added, and the ventilation and acoustics were improved. In 1940 the attic (third floor) was reconstructed and more space was made available. The English department left Rocky in 1932 and moved to Avery, when the music department took residence in Skinner.

For many Vassar students of the last seventy-five years, it all started when their teachers "filled" Rockefeller's "empty rooms with light."

36

The entrance to Rocky, 90 years later. With customary Rockefeller generosity to Vassar, which continues today, John D. built Vassar's first general academic building on a grand scale.

Rayfield

New England Building

By the turn of the century, the college needed a building to do for biology, physiology, and geology what Vassar Brothers Laboratory had done for physics and chemistry. After President Taylor failed to obtain an endowment, the New England alumnae, led by Florence Cushing, one of Vassar's three original alumnae trustees, went to work to raise the money. New England Building was the result, the second structure (Ely was the first) to be built through alumnae fund-raising. Moreover, a group of scientific buildings was soon planned for the south end of the campus. New England Building was placed between the recently built president's house (1896) and the old laboratory, with the thought that another chemistry building might take the skewed lab's place in future years.

The brick New England Building, like Rockefeller, was designed by York and Sawyer. With two stories, an attic, a basement, and a semicircular extension in the rear, it is graced by many large windows: five in Bedford stone and terracotta on the south side, two each on the east and west sides, and four on the north. The first floor was originally designated for geology, and the second for biology and physiology. A sweeping staircase winds up three stories to the top floor. (Newly refurbished, it is now more beautiful than ever.) Aaron L. Treadwell, professor of biology, was responsible for many of New England's modern features, including illumination by gas and provisions for electricity, which arrived on the Vassar campus in 1912. The light was so good, in any case, that microscopic work could be done either by daylight or gaslight.

The unfinished attic was altered in 1919 with the addition of dormer windows and several skylights. The remodeled space was used to create new quarters for the showcase specimens of birds and mammals that needed a home after the Museum had been converted into an assembly hall. According to head librarian Fanny Borden '98, who wrote about the New England alteration for the *Vassar Quarterly* in 1919: the "lighting and ventilation" were so much better in the new quarters that the collections "gained as much in attractiveness and usefulness as in accessibility."

Like several other Vassar buildings, New England has been used in a variety of unexpected ways over the years. The students taking biology exceeded the capacity of New England and Blodgett long before the branches of zoology, physiology, and plant science merged into a single biology department in 1964. Finally, in 1973, the biology department moved to Olmsted Hall where it could once again provide the kinds of conditions for teaching and research that students and faculty had enjoyed in the early years in New England Building.

At the present time, there is a wide range of departments and facilities in New England: the American Culture program, Women's Studies, Africana Studies, the Audio-Visual Resource Center, film-screening rooms and film office, studios for painting and sculpture, and the security office.

The fragment of Plymouth Rock encased over the front entrance still remains intact, although the geology department no longer occupies the building. It was brought to the campus from Plymouth, Massachusetts, by the indefatigable Cushing, a resident of nearby Norwood, who went to the rock and obtained a fragment when an accident made one available. These days her act would perhaps be considered irresponsible, but at the time it seemed the perfect gesture for a proud and unique building.

A fragment of Plymouth Rock

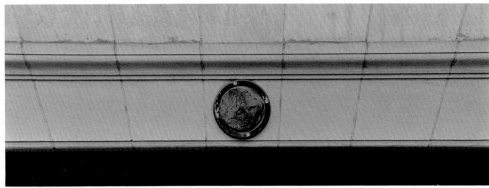

Sheridan

First illuminated by gas and equipped for biology, physiology, and geology, New England now houses the multi-disciplinary programs.

Sheridan

39

Sheridan

The semicircular extension, providing a lecture hall, is graced with five windows of terra cotta and Bedford stone.

The Chapel

The cloistered porch and entrance

Rayfield

41

On the first Saturday of October 1902, a ceremony was held to celebrate the new Vassar chapel. "How Firm a Foundation" and "The Church's One Foundation" made up the musical background as people gathered on the "Great South Lawn" to watch the laying of the cornerstone. President Taylor, joined by donors Mary Thaw Thompson and Mary Morris Pratt, read the list of documents embedded in the cornerstone and pressed it with mortar. The ceremony concluded with "Hark, Alma Mater" and symbolically ushered in a new era of endowed buildings.

The first plan was to build the chapel in the Gothic tradition. But there just wasn't enough room for such an elaborate edifice. So Charles Coolidge, the architect, discarded the Gothic design, and started afresh on the present Norman building.

Finding a proper location was difficult because the quadrangle had preempted the northern end of the campus. There were also problems with using a south lawn location: the ground fell away towards the lawn's periphery, and a large Gothic edifice, it was thought, would be placed too close to the central entrance leading from the gatehouse to Main. In addition, there were "unpleasant" cow and horse barns across the valley (where Skinner Hall was eventually built) that, it was feared, would mar the dignity of the building. (The problem was eliminated when the barns were moved to the "lower farm" near Hooker Avenue.)

Julia Ward Howe and a great academic procession, probably Vassar's first, helped mark the dedication of the new chapel on Friday, November 4, 1904. The choir contributed the music, and students and faculty lined up all over the campus, preparing for the march. The next day, the *New York Daily Tribune* described the latest Vassar building: "The new Chapel is of the Norman style of architecture, and is built of 'seamed' Cape Ann granite. The trimmings are of sandstone, the brownish color of the granite gives a beautiful warm effect. In the interior decorations, brown

relieved by dull gold, is the prevailing tone. There is much beautiful hand-carving in the woodwork, especially in the organ case and choir rails. The organ is one of the finest organs in any college chapel. It is provided with an Aeolian attachment."

Commemorative Tiffany and Dodge windows were later placed on the east side, John La Farge windows on the west side, and a Tiffany rose window over the north gable in the entrance archways.

The chapel was built by David MacLeod of D. C. Weeks, the firm that was then building St. John the Divine Cathedral in New York. It has a square, three-story tower on the northwest corner, and a semicircular, two-story wing to the south, with closed belfries on each side. Cloistered porches grace the north and east sides of the building, with five rounded arches and pillars on the north and four on the east. Five wooden double-doors with iron hinges open to the north.

After the chapel was built, the trustees decreed: "Owing to the situation of Main, the Chapel, Rockefeller, and the size of these buildings, the great lawns in front of Main should never be intruded upon by buildings." The trustees' dictum has actually been observed to this day. Taylor Hall and the library were subsequently placed on and near the street.

The chapel was (and still is) the largest religious edifice in Poughkeepsie. Although it has been altered, repaired, and acoustically improved, it is one of the few buildings that has not undergone considerable renovation. It can no longer hold the entire college community at one time, but, with the exception of Walker Field House, it remains the largest indoor gathering place on campus. Its use has gradually secularized as religious events have become somewhat more inclusive. The days of the hour-long Victorian sermons are no longer with us. The presidency of Henry Noble MacCracken marked the end of mandatory chapel attendance.

Sheridan

The building materials of the chapel combine Cape Ann granite, sandstone trim, and roof tile with Tiffany, Dodge, and La Farge stained-glass windows. ''Squeeze'' played its first American concert in the Vassar chapel.

Rayfield

43

Frederick Ferris Thompson Memorial Library

The Frederick Ferris Thompson Memorial Library has helped to define a Vassar education since it was built in 1905. Following the advice of such teachers as Lucy Maynard Salmon, Laura Wylie, Mabel Newcomer, and Helen Drusilla Lockwood '12, students have gone to the sources to find their answers rather than relying on textbooks. It has been said in many a class that the book you would find most interesting in the stacks would not be the book you thought you wanted, but rather the one *next* to it. The access to books provided by free entry into the stacks—the open stack system—has been one of the great features of Vassar's library and continues to be so despite the pressures for tighter security.

Matthew Vassar himself created the initial library collection; he contributed between three and four thousand of his own books, and a thousand purchased from Elias Magoon, when the college first opened. The original library was housed on the third floor of Main, opposite the chapel. After the 1893 Thompson Library Annex was added to Main Building, the library was moved and expanded. In 1905, Mary Clark Thompson endowed the new Frederick Ferris Thompson Memorial Library in memory of her husband, who had recently died.

The elaborately planned building was designed by Francis R. Allen and his associate Charles Collens of Boston in English Perpendicular style. With its massive central tower, three long wings, and entrance memorial hall, it faces Main Building, and lies across the lawn from the chapel (its companion in elegant detail). Constructed from Germantown stone, with Indiana limestone trimming, the building is decorated with tracery. To the front, off the great hall with its marble trim and fireplace, there are adjacent librarians' rooms; the hall also leads to galleries, seminar rooms, and the three radiating wings—west, north, and south.

The stained-glass window portraying the elevation of Elena Lucrezia Cornaro Piscopia to the Italian doctorate in 1678 is in the west wing. The window was designed in Birmingham, England, by Dunstan Powell, grandson of A. W. Pugin, the Victorian church architect. The much-debated question of whose idea it was to choose that subject has not been resolved. An unsigned October 1970 note in Special Collections reminds us that the colors of Elena Piscopia's costume, grey satin robes with a rose-lined overskirt, symbolize the dawn of women's higher education at Vassar.

A series of thirty-six leaded glass windows are placed in the tower. Stacks in the three wings provide open access to books. The collections gave disciplines other than the sciences their own laboratory. In fact, the *library* building became the laboratory as eleven seminar rooms or classrooms were incorporated into the design.

Between 1905 and 1916 the student population was reaching its capacity and both new and old disciplines needed more library space. By 1918, Mary Clark Thompson had provided two additional wings: a north addition that contained two rooms divided by bookstacks; and a south addition that contained three seminar rooms, a map room, a treasure room for Vassariana materials, the Turgenev collection, and manuscripts and rare books. Cloisters squared the angles formed by the wings and within the cloisters were two interior grassed courts. During the summer of 1918, after the addition was completed, Vassar student farmers in the War Emergency program transferred books into the new stacks, which provided space for 160,000 works and 600 readers.

Still, the need for library space continued. In 1925 the president

44

Rayfield

The Lockwood wing was added to Thompson in 1977 to include the Francis Fitz Randolph Rare Book Room, which now houses the Virginia B. Smith Manuscript Collection.

45

commented on that need and thereafter "some fourteen different sets of plans were drawn up and studied" before the designs for the Van Ingen addition were adopted by the trustees in 1934. For that construction, the Carnegie Corporation gave $160,000, and the trustees made available $160,000 more from the Thompson bequest to the college.

In 1961 the library was remodeled one more time through a gift from Elizabeth Stillman Williams '27. Shepley and Bulfinch were the architects. In this renovation the Gothic exterior of the building was not altered, but the interior was revamped to provide greater comfort and more efficiency for users and staff alike. The basement, which had contained an uninviting recess known to such researchers as those in Lockwood's press class as "the black hole of Calcutta," was made as efficient and attractive as the rest of the building. The two open courts were filled in; a cross walk bridged north and south portions of the second floor; the catalogue room was moved from the west wing to the south court, and a new loan desk was installed.

In 1977 the Lockwood wing, including the Francis Fitz Randolph Rare Book Room, provided improved resources for manuscript research, and more space for the library's growing collection of books, which now exceeds 600,000. Installed in the Lockwood wing is an all-night study room where students go without sleep while studying for exams and have access to terminals hooked up to Vassar's academic computer. During Virginia B. Smith's presidency, the college acquired the papers of Elizabeth Bishop '34 and Mary McCarthy '33, among others. There are now over eighty collections of women's papers to tempt researchers—Vassar students and more mature scholars alike—in the collection designated by the trustees as the Virginia B. Smith Manuscript Collection.

Rayfield

Thompson library, which Vassar students look to as the source, is often thought to be a cathedral by visitors.

46

Students' Building

In June 1901 Taylor reported on the progress of the college: "I have come to think that this social side needs an outward expression in a building which shall mark the common life and interest as distinguished from the intellectual work of the College. I have in mind an institution analogous to the Houston Club at the University of Pennsylvania or the new University Club at Harvard . . . Such a building, under proper control, would furnish reading rooms, lounging rooms, and the open fire, assembly rooms, committee rooms, and a sense of ownership and share in a building not devoted to college work but to college recreation."

With the accelerated decentralization of the campus and the increase in the student population in the first decade of the twentieth century, the need for such a building became urgent. Encouraged by the faculty to take responsibility for their own affairs, students formed new organizations and clubs, and even participated in intercollegiate events. More and more speakers like Gilbert Murray and William Butler Yeats came to lecture; Fritz Kreisler performed. But accommodations for socializing were cramped. Student life had outpaced Senior Parlor, the dances in J parlor, and the debates in Philaletheis Hall. Thus Students' Building, given by an anonymous donor later identified as Mary Babbott Ladd '08, was erected and made ready for use in 1913.

An issue of the *Miscellany News* from 1912 tells us that if the cornerstone ceremoniously sealed September 25 of that same year is ever opened, it will reveal the following items: an envelope containing the name of the donor and the reason for the gift; a student handbook for 1911-12; the constitutions for the Students' Association, the Athletic Association and the Philalethean Society; reports and by-laws of the Christian Association; a printed statement regarding the maids' clubhouse (Good Fellowship Club); a catalogue of the college for 1911-12; a plan of the grounds at the time of construction of the building; a copy of the *Miscellany News* for July 1912; extracts from the *Miscellany News* for October, November, and December of 1902, when the Students' Association was formally reorganized and chartered; a list from the *Vassarion* of 1912 naming organizations existing at Vassar from 1861 to 1911; the names of then existing organizations, presidents, and officers of various associations and classes; a card stating that it is the wish of the donor that the building be known as Students' Building; and another, stating that Bishop and Company are the builders, and McKim, Mead, and White of New York are the architects.

Joseph Herenden Clark, an eager new young architect in the firm, speaks in his autobiography of being told that the structure should be of brick with a slate roof and white trim. He thought almost immediately of a building studied during his then recent days at Columbia School of Architecture—Christ Church, George Washington's church in Alexandria, Virginia. He decided to go to Virginia and study its details inside and outside. His design for Students' Building, his first public building, was drawn up with Christ Church in mind.[5]

As designed, the building consisted of two stories and a basement. It had a simple but impressive facade with wooden pillars, pediment, and cupola. Several outside steps led to a central entrance, with a set of large double doors, and two smaller ones. There were three identical windows above the doors. The interior of the building contained space for basement offices, a large auditorium with a stage, and meeting rooms on each

47

Rayfield

Made into the All College Dining Center, and quickly dubbed ACDC, in 1973, Students' Building was known to decades of Vassar students as the place for junior prom, the bicycle exchange, faculty follies, the *Miscellany News* **office, or Judicial Board hearings.**

side of the auditorium for student organizations. On the second floor was a rectangular-shaped balcony following the lines of the auditorium, and a formal meeting place for small student groups called the Old Council Room. The Students' Association had been granted a new charter in 1902, and the Students' Building provided the urgently needed space for the many extracurricular activities that were still next-to-roomless in 1912. Philaletheis, for example, had originally been granted space in the Calisthenium, and subsequently in the Alumnae Gym, but as the college expanded there were many conflicting demands for existing space, and Philaletheis had been squeezed out.

Occasions like the Junior Prom were celebrated on the dance floor and in the alcoves of Students', while freshmen and sophomores watched the president of the class and her date lead the grand march. The basement housed a bicycle exchange, a shop for second-hand books, and miscellaneous storage of trunks and boxes. Whenever a secular speaker was expected to draw a large audience, the event would be held in Students' as the chapel was only used for more solemn occasions. Once a year the faculty put on Founder's Day skits for the students. On one memorable occasion Professor C. Gordon Post brought down the house when he and his colleagues in political science enacted a scene from *Little Women*. Clair Leonard and Homer Pearson played jazz duets on twin pianos, and Sarah Blanding dressed up as Edith Sitwell, flipping pages of her lecture.

In 1945 at the end of World War II, the building was partially reconstructed and redecorated. More recreational space was needed and a student eating place called "The Hoot" was newly located in the west corridor. The Old Council Room was also redecorated and repainted.

Until 1973 students ate in their individual dorms, with some of the food being cooked on the spot and other food delivered by truck from the bakeries and kitchens in the basement of Jewett. Even before the student population reached the ceiling of 2,250, college authorities had been searching for ways to facilitate food service more economically. Gone were the days of elegant dining on table linen with maid service in the halls. Self-service and "scrape" were instituted during the war, and the college was never to return to its previous luxury. Plans for a central dining plant that would link the quad houses were eventually abandoned. Finally, after the college had become coeducational, the Town Houses and Terrace Apartments were built (1971 and 1972), Students' was remodeled to become the All College Dining Center in 1973.

The $3.5 million central dining hall was designed by Walker O. Cain and Associates, a firm descended from McKim, Mead, and White. Friends and relatives of Mary Babbott Ladd, the original donor, contributed over one million dollars to the building's renovation, and several special rooms were created or furnished through other gifts. Although the cupola and columns remain, two small red brick wings were added at either side. The interior, according to a college news release, was redesigned "to achieve maximum flexibility in use and to retain as much as possible of the warm atmosphere of the old house dining rooms." There are eight separate dining rooms on the east side of the building—seven small ones and one medium sized—and a small and large dining area on the west side. Upstairs one can find the dishwashing equipment and offices for the staff. These days it is not unusual to wander ACDC's halls and run into chefs trained by the C.I.A. (Culinary Institute of America), a Poughkeepsie neighbor.

Taylor Hall

The plain truth is that the whole building is a Gothic conspiracy of design for beauty and use, surprise and strangeness, complexity and utility.
—Henry Noble MacCracken, as quoted by Charles M. Pratt, 1915, from an account of the Taylor Hall dedication

Taylor Hall, built for the study of art, was given by Charles M. and Mary Morris Pratt to honor their close friend president emeritus James Monroe Taylor. The hall joined the library and the chapel as one of three elegant, endowed buildings constructed after 1900 for specialized use.

The building was dedicated on Founder's Day, 1915, and Taylor was the chief speaker as well as the honored guest. In his speech, he emphasized that when Vassar first opened there had not been a college in America, with the possible exception of Harvard and Rochester, that considered art education worthy of collegiate study. He traced his own interest in art education to the time when he had been a student at the University of Rochester and would attend President Martin B. Anderson's Saturday morning lectures on great painters and engravers. Taylor also pointed out that many of Vassar's charter trustees were significant members of the art world, such as Anderson; Benson Lossing, an engraver of note; Samuel F. B. Morse, a well-known painter; and Elias Magoon, an art collector. In fact Matthew Vassar had bought Magoon's collection for the college at a price of $20,000.

Because men's colleges in the 1860s did not offer art education, the Vassar trustees were reluctant, Taylor speculated, to make music and painting part of the regular curriculum. Instead, "schools were formed for special students of the arts," and college students who had the time could join classes for an extra fee. Main was equipped with a large studio, where a variety of lectures on art were offered, and students could be awarded a separate diploma for three years of work in the school of painting. Henry Van Ingen, a painter "discovered" in Rochester by Anderson, and whose self-portrait is in the Taylor Hall collection, presided over the painting division from the opening of college until his death in 1898.

Before 1886, Taylor recalled, the art department had been moved to the riding academy, despite "the danger of fire." For Vassar was poor: "how poor none of you will ever know who has not [had] to find friends and funds to meet the elementary needs of the college," he remarked. The riding academy was the best the college could do. Yet Taylor had always felt that art and music should be integrated into the main curriculum. So when Professor Frederick Louis Ritter of the Music School died in 1891, Taylor recommended to the trustees that art and music become part of the regular course of study and that the standards in these disciplines be equal to those in other departments. This elimination of the special students proved to be a considerable step in the strengthening of Vassar's academic program.

Taylor Hall stands at the gateway of the college, taking the place of the former Renwick gate lodge that was destroyed to make room for it. A two-story Gothic structure, Taylor Hall is made from soft brown granite and Indiana limestone. As classicist Elizabeth Hazelton Haight '94 noted in a 1915 article, like Thompson Library, it is decorated with sculpture such as "the figures of artists, the mocking gargoyles, the seals of nations, Athens' owl and Rome's wolf on either side of the great entrance gate."[6] The first floor area embraces an entry way for vehicles with two foot passages on either side. Originally there were gatekeeper's quarters (at least temporarily occupied by Professor Haight) on the north side,

A gift of the Pratt family, this "Gothic conspiracy" is to be enlarged by the end of the 1980s.

Sheridan

Sheridan

Sheridan

51

facing, on the south side, a large marble entrance hall and staircase. Connecting with the end of the hall was a lecture room which, with its raked floor and tiny electric lights, became over time the most familiar lecture hall on the Vassar campus. Through the years Art 105 students have listened there to the memorable slide lectures of Agnes Rindge Claflin, Leila Barber, Adolph Katzenellenbogen, Richard Krautheimer, and their successors. The second floor originally contained painting and sculpture exhibition rooms and the large gallery over the lecture hall was to be used as a college reception room. In 1922 the casts of sculpture which, with the Ghiberti door casts had been moved to Taylor from Avery in 1914 at the building's opening, were removed from the Gallery, which was subsequently redecorated, yielding a permanent place for loan exhibitions.

In 1937 the Van Ingen addition connected Thompson Library to Taylor Hall, thereby uniting the art library with the central library. It provides a three-level stack with stalls and small studies to accommodate one hundred more readers. There are also a number of rooms located above and adjacent to the stacks: the art library, seminar rooms, a slide room, a photograph room, and the librarian's office. Above the art library, one can find a drafting room for students of architecture, a conference room, and a room for projecting slides.

The Van Ingen wing was one of the first buildings of its kind in the United States. The reconstruction was designed by Allen, Collens, and Willis, and by Theodore Muller, collaborating with Professor John McAndrew of both the Vassar department and the Museum of Modern Art. The desire for a functional design led to the use of glass brick for partitions, and to lighting and decorating that enables art objects to be displayed in their true colors.

Sheridan

The familiar Gothic arch took the place of Renwick's original entrance and is captured in sterling on Elizabeth Jones's medal for the President's Distinguished Visitors.

52

Blodgett Hall of Euthenics

The idea in presenting to euthenics the whole quadrangular space upon the old campus, roughly called the old tennis courts, is because this building will be a really noble building of considerable size and of very great importance from the educational point of view.
—Henry Noble MacCracken to Charles Collens, college supervising architect, October 19, 1923

Another, and also familiar, Gothic arch

Sheridan

Blodgett Hall of Euthenics had been in the works ever since the young Henry Noble MacCracken officially assumed office in October 1915. The building, a gift of Minnie Cumnock Blodgett '84 and her husband, John Wood Blodgett, was not built, however, until 1928. At MacCracken's inauguration, Julia Lathrop '80, founder of the government's Children's Bureau, gave a persuasive speech entitled "The Highest Profession for Women." In it she urged that women be educated and trained in the new discipline of euthenics, a word coined by Ellen Swallow Richards '70, a Vassar graduate who pioneered in family life. Minnie Blodgett, Julia Lathrop, and Ellen Richards worked together to urge the young, progressive, ambitious, and somewhat vulnerable president to make euthenics part of the curriculum of the social sciences. The euthenics program, which was instituted in 1924, was never well received by the Vassar faculty. In fact, some members, such as Margaret Floy Washburn '91 and Mabel Newcomer, considered it a step backward, reintroducing in modern guise the notion that women's place was in the home.

Matthew Vassar himself had been very committed to the subject of domestic economy. In fact in his last speech before the board of trustees, the founder collapsed and died before having had a chance to explain why he thought the controversial topic should be incorporated into the college's curriculum.

Neither the early presidents nor the trustees, however, shared Matthew Vassar's commitment to domestic science. For example, although Presidents Raymond, Caldwell, and Taylor acknowledged a difference in objectives between education for men and women, they emphasized that this difference was not to be reflected in academic subject matter: men and women were to study the same subjects. But the debate did not end here. MacCracken took it a step further. He believed that euthenics, the science of bettering living conditions, was a promising field for women to study and to employ both in the communities in which they lived and in their professions. Although euthenics was not quite the *scientific* discipline that Matthew Vassar had imagined, MacCracken still viewed it as a latter-day, but much expanded, embodiment of the founder's dream.

Perhaps more than any other building on campus Blodgett Hall spoke to an *idea*. It incorporated under one roof facilities for lectures, laboratory work, museum displays, household technology, as well as library resources for the social sciences. Indeed, according to MacCracken in a letter to the architect, its object was to include "the sciences which have to do with the improvement of material living conditions, and its landscape and general design" were to be "in harmony with this purpose." Thus the building originally provided rooms for a variety of such uses: applied chemistry, mental hygiene, statistics and mechanical drawing, applied physiology, interior decoration and design, applied economics, and geography.

The building, as MacCracken indicated, opened up a new area of the campus. The trustees had acquired Wing Farm to the northeast of the regular campus and decided to develop it, under the direction of Keene Richards, the new general manager, and Charles Collens, supervising

53

architect, into a quadrangular group opening to the east. Such an orientation would take advantage of the view of Sunset Hill and the beautiful Pine Walk of "superb trees" (still there today). Blodgett was to be the key unit in the group which would include a nursery school, a gymnasium, and a freshman dormitory, all dedicated to improved living.

Indeed, the early Blodgett was more than simply an academic building. In the 1920s the director of euthenics, chemistry professor Anne Louise MacLeod, cooperated with a trustee committee headed by Minnie Blodgett and students working in the euthenics program, to assess and reform dietary provisions on the Vassar campus. In the 1930s the first group of cooperative students lived together in Blodgett South. In the 1940s Helen Lockwood, professor of English, and Clarice Pennock '19, director of field work, instituted a social museum in Blodgett that exhibited results of Vassar's work in the Poughkeepsie community. And during the thirties and forties the Vassar Summer Institute of Euthenics attracted students and their families to summer sessions held in Blodgett and elsewhere on campus. (This was Vassar's second summer school, the first having been the School for Nurses in the summer of 1918, also promoted by Mrs. Blodgett.)

After the '40s, and especially with biology's move to Olmsted, the hall dedicated to euthenics became a building of more general use. (In fact, physiology had occupied the north wing since 1938.) But the many children who still play in Wimpfheimer's three playgrounds carry on the spirit of their predecessors who were admitted to share the campus in 1927 as part of an American college's first fully developed program in child study, a program now incorporated into the psychology department curriculum.

Sheridan

54

Blodgett, late
afternoon,
summer 1986

55

Dexter M. Ferry Cooperative House

Marcel Breuer offered his "first and only" poem at the dedication of Ferry House on October 5, 1951:
"Often you ask: where and how and what are Aesthetics, beyond functions needed?
Colors which you can hear with ears;
Sounds to see with eyes;
The void you touch with your elbow;
The taste of space on your tongue;
The fragrance of dimensions;
The juice of stone."

Twenty-seven students took up housekeeping in the exciting and colorful "bi-nuclear" Ferry House that fall. The building, made of painted white brick, is contrasted with the adjacent red brick of Avery and Main. A dormitory on two levels, the ground floor provides common rooms for housekeeping and socializing and the elevated area offers combined bedroom and study accommodations. Now that the modern and functional College Center has created a new nerve center behind Main, and the brick and limestone Seeley G. Mudd building has been built as an exciting neighbor, Ferry House no longer seems remote and separate.

Ferry House was given by Dexter M. Ferry of Detroit, brother of Blanche Ferry Hooker '99 and Queene Ferry Coonley '96, who together gave Vassar Alumnae House in 1924. Dexter Ferry also had two Vassar daughters—Edith Ferry Hooper '32 and Jean Ferry Davis '35—as well as a daughter-in-law and five nieces who attended Vassar. In his dedicatory remarks he noted that he had been struck during his early Vassar visits by the scarcity of food on campus for guests like himself. The well-equipped cooperative Ferry House kitchen would, it was hoped, assure better luck for male visitors of the fifties.

As a cooperative, Ferry House was not without precedent. The first Vassar cooperative students set up housekeeping in Blodgett in the 1930s. When Blodgett was absorbed by other uses, the old Wing Farm House was then remodeled to become a cooperative called Palmer House (1938). The distances, however, proved too great—longer than a ten minute walk from Blodgett (or Palmer House) to Skinner—and cooperative living was temporarily abandoned until (precipitated by the exigencies of World War II when students took over household tasks in dormitories) it emerged again in Ferry.

Ferry House, together with Noyes and Chicago Hall (1959), were all added to the campus during the years in office of Sarah Gibson Blanding, Vassar's first woman president, who previously had been dean of the School of Home Economics at Cornell. There had not been such prolific building activities on campus for twenty years, for her endeavors in this decade as well rebuilt Davison House, damaged by fire on March 16, 1959, and Main, in need of both remodeling and restoration.

In Ferry provisions were made for a housefellow's apartment. (In Noyes there were two.) The housefellow program, launched as an experiment in 1951 under the auspices of a gift from Paul Mellon (through the Old Dominion Foundation) relieved faculty members of one third of their normal teaching load, thus allowing them to spend time fostering cultural and intellectual life in student dormitories. Anna Odor Buchholz, then an instructor of German, now supervisor of the Town of Poughkeepsie, was the first Noyes house fellow.

Students living in Ferry today still save over $2,500 on their board and room through performing their own household management duties.

56

Sheridan

Marcel Breuer's design for a cooperative dormitory, Ferry is nestled between Avery and Main, with the always visible smokestack behind it.

Belle Skinner Hall of Music

Rayfield

In Skinner are 27 private studios and a composer's retreat.

The department as a whole continues to grow and the question of an adequate building is more and more pressing. For many years the music department at Vassar has been more poorly housed than that of any other of the important women's colleges, while its work has compared favorably with them all. In these rooms, badly heated, lighted, and ventilated, and without proper sound-proofing, there has accumulated valuable teaching equipment, of instruments and library, much of it irreplaceable in case of fire.
—Alice Snyder '09, professor of English, writing in the *Vassar Quarterly* about the need for a music building in 1923

Skinner Hall was given to the college in 1932 by William Skinner, president of Skinner & Son, silk manufacturers of Holyoke, Massachusetts, in honor of Belle Skinner, his sister, the president of the class of 1887. (Two older sisters had preceded her at Vassar: Nancy Skinner |Clark| of the class of 1875 and Elizabeth Skinner |Hubbard| of the class of 1880.)

Classical music was Belle Skinner's first love; but after World War I, she also devoted herself to the restoration of Hattonchatel, a ruined medieval village in France. In 1927 she established the Belle Skinner Fellowship, enabling Vassar students to study history in French provincial universities—a fellowship later augmented by her brother.

Skinner borders the southern end of campus, at a discreet distance from the Norman medieval chapel and the English Gothic Taylor Hall. According to Dean Ella McCaleb '78, Taylor had written that a building for music was "corollary to his belief in the importance of developing the aesthetic side of the college course." Yet when Henry Sanders wanted to give a music building in 1909, Taylor channeled his gift to chemistry instead.

When the chapel was dedicated, Taylor declared that the hill in back of it covered by barns was the "inevitably suitable site" for the music hall. Every year thereafter he urged that "barn hill" be made ready for the new building.

Skinner is a tribute to the hard work and meticulous thinking of George Sherman Dickinson, known as "Dicky" to several generations of Vassar students. Not an architect, he nonetheless planned the interior of the building and all its rooms, including the medieval setting on the third floor used for the instrument collection. The bona fide architect was Charles Collens of Boston, who also designed Riverside Church in New York City.

Skinner has three units or wings adjoining one another to form a square-cornered U, with room for a formal garden in the open court. (The garden never materialized.) The north wing contains a recital lecture hall, with a ceiling reminiscent of the Loire Valley. The center unit consists of classrooms, offices, and studios; the south section, acoustically perfected practice rooms. The building stands against the hillside—four stories high on the campus side and three stories along Raymond Avenue. It can be approached by a picturesque bridge across the Casperkill Creek, separating the site from the campus proper. It was originally hoped that Skinner, like Taylor Hall, would be available to Poughkeepsie residents.

The lecture/recital hall, constantly used by the music faculty, students, and outside artists and groups, seats 500 people and stretches two and one-half stories to the vaulted ceiling. It was designed to permit daylight on three sides, and provide instrument storage below. There is a composer's retreat—Thekla Hall—on the fourth floor; and twenty-seven private practice rooms or studios to insure concentration.

Dickinson also planned the Skinner library, which has lent further distinction to the music department; although among colleges, Vassar had always been a leader in music education. In 1891 Vassar set the standard in undergraduate arts education by making music a regular, not special, department.

Vassar set the standard in undergraduate arts education in 1891 by making art and music regular departments.

Rayfield

Kenyon Hall

Designs for proposed buildings have been the subject of many Vassar controversies—Seeley G. Mudd, Walker Field House, and the Lockwood addition to the library. None, however, compares with the controversy in 1932 over the design for the Kenyon Hall of Physical Education.

The trouble began when a campaign to raise $500,000 for a new gymnasium used a prospectus with a sketch of the suggested building that was said to look like Matthew Vassar's birthplace in Norfolk, England. In fact it did not. Vassar's birthplace was much less grand.

"The general scheme [was] to be of an English country house with farm buildings suitable to the landscape," the prospectus announced. The design for the modified Gothic building struck the editors of the *Miscellany News* and some members of the college community as outlandish. Before plans for the building could be completed, a full-blown debate on "false expression" in architecture had been waged in the campus press.

The college had certainly outgrown the old Alumnae Gymnasium, and a new athletic facility was urgently needed. As part of the development of the Wing Farm section of the campus (purchased in 1922), the Helen Kenyon Gymnasium was designed to provide a much more far-reaching and comprehensive athletic program. It was to be a laboratory where the art of physical development would be learned thoroughly so as to be practiced throughout life by every alumna, as William Darrach, M.D., said at its dedication.

Alice Belding, professor of physical education from 1926 to 1937, was largely responsible for the internal design of Kenyon Hall. She visited new gymnasiums throughout the country and worked with the architect so that Kenyon would meet the academic needs of the department as well as the recreational needs of students and their male guests—"a new idea," according to the faculty minutes memorializing Belding's death in 1960.

Plans for the building called for both a southern and eastern elevation of cut stone (to match the nursery school and Blodgett Hall of Euthenics), and northern and western faces of brick. According to the prospectus, the building would emphasize the "pleasure of exercise" rather than the "duty of taking it." The swimming pool "would look like safe anchorage for all the navies of the world." Twenty-two windows would let sun into the swimming pool area; there would be ample room available for individual work with students; the dressing rooms would be light and airy; and there would be an indoor tennis court, squash courts, and a handball court. Like its predecessor the Calisthenium, Kenyon would have a bowling alley. It would even have a solarium on an internal flat roof for sunbathing. And on the west back side, there would be a massive court for basketball.

Nancy G. Rodman '32, an editor of the *Miscellany News*, wrote vehemently about the proposed gymnasium. She asked: "Do we want another Old World post-Gothic building on the campus? Are we satisfied to live in an atmosphere of antiquity. . . when our minds and activities should be with our age? Are we satisfied to view the outer world through mullioned windows. . .?" Rodman also called for a "new modern style. . .with an abundance of air, sunlight, and freedom. . .not a roost for the birds and a barrier for English fog." Other opinions were voiced in the debate that ensued. Winifred Smith '04, professor of drama who "didn't mind being quoted," also participated in the debate by congratulating students for their "splendidly cogent protests against the dominance of Collegiate Gothic on our campus and in America."

An anonymous letter-writer in a subsequent issue of the newspaper wrote that the "complicated wing in the foreground with peaked dormers and . . .gables [looked as though it could house] at least three apartments and several stories rather than only one swimming pool!" Because of the leaded panes of glass, another commentator wrote, "It will be like swimming in a sort of Alice in Wonderland transformation of a don's private study." Still a third writer said: "And that left front wing, which seems to be an Olde Half Timberede Englishe Inn on One Side and a forsaken abbey on the other—what is that? Offices, it would appear—and Corrective exercises, on the first floor. Fencing, among the half-timbers and gables and dizzy roof slopes. Dancing, under the chimney (apparently a fake) and in and out of the little bird bath oriel. [The tennis court would be] lost in that charming disarray of crumbling barns, leaning stables and murky hay-lofts."

After much further debate, Charles Collens, then general consulting architect to the college, announced that the plans had been modified. The half-timbered work and the fake chimney would be removed. The oriel would be replaced with a large area of glass, changing the entire service end of the building to brick and steel construction. Large panes of factory glass would be used to light the tennis court and pool area, thus leaving the south front, including the street side of the swimming pool, the only "frankly Gothic" area. In this way, Kenyon would harmonize with Blodgett, even though the building material had been altered from stone to brick.

(An irony not mentioned, and perhaps not broadly known, was that when Matthew Vassar commissioned Frederick Rondel, a Hudson River painter, to paint his English birthplace, it was portrayed as a one-story cottage.)

Sheridan

Vassar's third, but not last, gymnasium, had an outdoor solarium and was to emphasize the pleasure of exercise rather than the duty of taking it.

62

Rayfield

The field house, sited between two playing fields and opposite the Terrace Apartments, has become an active center for physical fitness and social life.

Walker Field House

With the coeducational student body reaching approximately 2,250, Kenyon could no longer meet the demand for athletic space. So in 1982 the Walker Field House, designed by Daniel F. Tully Associates, was built.

On September 25, 1982, Margaret Walker Spofford '26, Margaret Spofford Benkard '61, and Nancy Spofford Yerkes '52 presided over the opening of the field house which they had partially endowed with two other family members, Shaw Walker and the late Jane Walker McKinney '24.

The field house accommodates basketball, tennis, volleyball, and a running track. The large natatorium, with a movable bulkhead separating diving and swimming areas, increases the college's recreational as well as team facilities. This new swimming pool is to the pool in Kenyon what the pool in Kenyon was to the pool in the Alumnae Gym. There are, however, no leaded windows, nor, indeed, any windows at all.

The Calisthenium, along with materials supplied by the system of Dio Lewis, was once the last word in calisthenics. Now Walker provides nine Eagle and Nautilus machines that, according to a timely flier in campus mailboxes, exercise every muscle of the body. These days, of course, students write their own exercise regimen. But they are now joined by other members of the college community who also use the building in a new kind of camaraderie. Some say the machine room has become "the spot," more popular, perhaps, than the Retreat in the College Center. Finding it much easier to go there for a cup of coffee, however, this writer will have to admit that that is only hearsay.

Seeley G. Mudd Chemistry Building

Sheridan

Sheridan

64

Technical innovations in 1984 included solar heating, a central duct system, and research labs adjoining faculty offices. The glass facade on the south (left photo) collects heat while the brick facade on the north (right photo) repels cold.

Seeley G. Mudd, like its predecessors, became one of the most technologically advanced chemistry buildings in the country. Just as Benjamin Silliman, Jr., and Leroy Cooley had been concerned with functionalism, safety, space, light, and protection from noxious fumes and contaminants in 1879, so were the architects of Mudd.

Mudd, however, is as different from Sanders as Sanders was from Vassar Brothers Laboratory. In Sanders, solid brick walls cut the building up into unalterable spaces so that the size of rooms was set. In Mudd, however, there are no partitions in the work spaces, so, there are no barriers to flexibility. In Sanders, work that required control of vapors had to be done in the "stink room" under a hood. In Mudd, *all* work in organic chemistry is done under hoods.

Standing more or less where Vassar Brothers Laboratory once stood, Mudd has been designed with reference to the buildings around it—especially to Main. Mudd completes the science quadrangle, which now consists of New England Building, Sanders Classroom, and Sanders Physics. Vassar's science buildings actually formed a skewed quadrangle once before, between 1926 and 1938—after Sanders Physics was built and before Vassar Brothers was razed. A building similar to Blodgett was proposed in 1915 to house physics and psychology and to be located across the service road behind the chapel near where Olmsted now stands. But Sanders Physics became the choice in 1926. In fact when the site was chosen for Olmsted, between New England and Sanders Physics, it became a kind of pentagonal growth on the quadrangle.

It was first proposed that the new chemistry building be placed towards the glen and open-air theater below Sanders Physics. Various environmental problems interfered with the first choice; and the building was finally placed at the north end of the quadrangle, where it now stands.

Mudd, whose colors blend with the neighboring buildings, uses brick, limestone, and glass as exterior decoration. It has three levels, with the first two floors used principally for laboratory space and the ground floor for offices, material preparation for classes, and storage. The southern facade of the building faces Sanders Physics, and the elevation has inner brick and outer glass walls. Air space between the two is heated by the sun and the resulting warm air enters the main building through ducts. The laboratories are vented by a central duct system, removing fumes through the missile-shaped outlets that seem to rise from the building towards space.

The major gift towards the $7.2 million cost of the building came from the Seeley G. Mudd Fund. Perry, Dean, Rogers and Partners of Boston were the architects, and a separate New York firm, Dubin-Bloome Associates, designed the energy features.

One can look at Mudd from any vantage point and enjoy a feast of glass, brick, sunlight, color, and animation. Not everyone approves of the building on first sight, or even after quite some time. But it has already been the subject of a cover article in the April 1986 edition of *Architectural Record*; and it joins several other campus buildings as a work of architectural distinction.

At the formalities celebrating the opening of the building in September 1985, Linus Pauling gave a lecture on nutrition, and chemistry majors from past years offered a feast of papers.

Matthew Vassar, almost always open-minded and ready for change, as noted by Maria Mitchell after he died, would probably have rejoiced to have such an advanced building as Mudd on his campus in time for the 125th anniversary of the founding of his college. It's hard to guess, however, what his less imaginative nephew Matthew Vassar, Jr., would have thought of the most recent replacement of his laboratory.

Rayfield

66

Mudd, placed on the site of Vassar's first science building, completes a quadrangle with Sanders Classroom, Sanders Physics, and New England.

Sheridan

67

Vassar College Buildings, 1865-1986

In 1986 an inventory of Vassar buildings includes: 37 academic, administrative, and major service buildings; 10 dormitories; 9 terrace apartments; 15 town houses; 4 major faculty apartment buildings; 2 off-campus houses for student housing; 16 Vassar-owned single houses; 12 faculty apartments (including 6 Watson apartment buildings); 20 miscellaneous structures; 60 faculty-owned houses on college property—a total of 185 buildings. In addition, 2 buildings have been torn down. At least 4 buildings have had fires causing considerable damage. Building records of the college are incomplete and sometimes hard to track down.

The list given below excludes privately owned houses built on college property after 1930, and also privately owned houses on college property acquired after 1960. Houses, like other buildings, have been both recycled and changed hands. Buildings are named as they are listed initially in building records.

This list is adapted from one found in Special Collections, dated December 7, 1959. It has been correlated with existing records in the Facilities Planning offices.

Building	Architect	Date Completed
Alumnae Gymnasium (Ely Hall)	William M. Tubby	1889
Additions (1906, 1933, 1937)	William Downing	1906
Alumnae House	Hunt & Hunt	1924
Aubrey House (159 College)	Edward C. Smith	1926
Baldwin House (168 College)	Copied. No architect	1916
Baldwin Infirmary	Faulkner & Kingsbury	1940
Barbour House (166 College)	Ruth Adams	1922
Barn (Cow) North Section	Vassar College designed	1901
Barn (Cow) East Section	Vassar College designed	1907
Barn (Cow) West Section	Vassar College designed	1909
Barn (Horse)	Vassar College designed	1922
Blodgett Hall	York & Sawyer	1928
Boiler House	Frank Sutton	1917
Booth House (153 College)	H. F. Mueller	1914
Booth House Studio (153 College)	Edward C. Smith	1930
Borden House (3 Orchard La.)	Richard M. Bennett	1941
Burling House (136 Fulton)	L. L. Booth	1926
Calisthenium and Riding Academy	J. A. Wood	1866
Remodeled and renamed: Museum (1875); Assembly Hall (1918); Avery (1931)		
Chapel	Shepley, Rutan & Coolidge	1904
Chicago Hall	Schweikher & Elting	1959
Chicken House (old)	Vassar College	1916
Chicken House (new)	Vassar College	1926
Chimney	Alphonse Custodis	1908
Coal Bunkers	Frank Sutton	1921
Coal Pockets	Vassar College	1902
Conservation Greenhouse	Lord & Burnham	1940
Corn Crib	Vassar College	1917

Cottages

A Cottage (87 Raymond)	Francis R. Allen	1891
B Cottage (85 Raymond)	Francis R. Allen	1892
C Cottage (83 Raymond)	Francis R. Allen	1892
D Cottage (81 Raymond)	Francis R. Allen	1892
Creamery	Vassar College	1910
Creamery Addition	Vassar College	1938
Creamery Washroom	Vassar College	1926
Cushing House	Allen & Collens	1927
Davison House	Allen & Vance	1902
Dean's House (172 College)	Ruth Adams	1932
Dedrick House (corner Hooker; moved to near Rombout)		1900
D'Luhosch (Blegen House)		
Doctor's Garage	Faulkner & Kingsbury	1940
Doughty House (Rombout)		1860
Addition		1923
Drake House (170 College)	Rollin S. Tuttle	1915
Duggan House (Wing Farm)	Gindele & Johnson	1970
Eleanor Conservatory		1886
Eleanor Plant Science Lab.	Lord & Burnham	1941
Farm Double House (East of Cow Barn) Razed, 1970s	Vassar College	1902
Feeder House (at Chicken Houses)		1926
Ferry House	Marcel Breuer	1951
Ferrell House (166A College) (Chaplain's House)	Goldstone & Dearborn	1958
Fire Pump House		1865
Flagler House (Child-Care Cooperative)		1917
Garage, College Ave. (Pumping)	Vassar College	1907
Garage and Shop	Vassar College	1930
Garage, South of Boiler Shop	E. C. Anderson	1915
Gate Lodge (razed 1914)	James Renwick, Jr.	1865
Goodfellowship Clubhouse (Maid's Clubhouse)	Pilcher & Tachau	1908
Gow House (147 College)		1907
Green Pastures (Thelberg Road)		1820
Greenhouse (East Section)	Lord & Burnham	1937
Greenhouse (Center Section)		1938
Hill House (77 Raymond)	Pilcher & Tachau	1904
Hinkle House (160 College)		1890
Howell House (East of Cow Barns)		1917
Hughes Farm House		1926
Imer House (155 College)	Edward C. Smith	1927
Josselyn House	Allen & Collens	1912
Kendrick House	York & Sawyer	1927
Kenyon Hall	Allen & Collens	1933
Keys House (151 College)		1907
Lathrop House	Allen & Vance	1901

Laundry	James Post	1872
West Addition	Vassar College	1901
East Addition	Vassar College	1909
Alteration to Computer Center		1966
Leach House (75 Raymond)	H. B. Russell	1910
Lutz House (La Grange)		
Lyman House (151 College)	Percival M. Lloyd	1907
Main Building	James Renwick, Jr.	1865
Extension, dining room and kitchen	James S. Post	1872
Thompson Annex	Francis R. Allen	1893 — library
Kitchen and Dining Room Reconstruction	Allen & Collens	1918
Remodeling ground floor	John McAndrew	1937
Remodeling, removal of Annex	Goldstone & Dearborn	1959
College Center	Jean Carlhian, Shepley, Bulfinch, Richardson and Abbott	1977
Matzig House (Collegeview)	Charles Cooke	1932
McCaleb House (71 Raymond)	Allen & Collens	1912
Metcalf House	York & Sawyer	1915
Seeley G. Mudd Chemistry Building	Perry, Dean, Rogers & Partners	1984
Murphy Farm Apartments	Legendre, Johnson & McNeil	1984
New England Building	York & Sawyer	1901
Alteration		1919
North Hall (Pilcher's Crime)	Pilcher & Tachau	1907
Renamed Jewett		1915
Noyes House	Eero Saarinen	1958
Observatory	Charles S. Farrar	1864
Addition		1895
Olmsted Hall	Sherwood Mills & Smith (SMS)	1972
Outdoor Theater		1916
Palmer House (two old barns remodeled to Wing Farm House)	Edward C. Smith	1927
East Wing Addition	Faulkner & Kingsbury	1938
Peirce House (162 College)	Edward C. Smith	1927
Piggery	Vassar College	1904
Power House	Haughevont Co. of N.Y.	1864
Power House	Lord & Co.	1912
Powerhouse Theater	Robertson Wood, Jr.	1973
Pratt House	York & Sawyer	1916
President's House	Rossiter & Wright	1895
Raymond House	Francis R. Allen	1897
Riley House (73 Raymond)	Edward C. Smith	1912
Rockefeller Hall	York & Sawyer	1897
Enlarged		1916
		1940
Rombout House Garage	Vassar College	1925
Sanders Chemistry (Sanders Classroom)	Ewing & Chappelle	1909
Sanders Physics	Ewing & Allen	1926

71

Service Building	Vassar College	1925
Sewer Pump House	Vassar College	1925
Skinner "Head House"	Hutchins, Evans & Lefferts	1984
Skinner Hall	Allen & Collens	1932
Strong Hall	Francis R. Allen	1893
Students' Building	McKim, Mead & White	1913
Reconstruction ACDC	Walker O. Cain & Assoc.	1973
Swift Infirmary	York & Sawyer	1900
Remodeled		1941
Tabard		
Taylor Hall	Allen & Collens	1915
Terrace Apartments	Shepley, Bulfinch, Richardson & Abbott	1972
Terry House (157 College)	Dubois Carpenter	1910
Frederick Ferris Thompson		
Memorial Library	Allen & Collens	1905
Wings	Allen & Collens	1918
Reconstruction	Shepley & Bulfinch	1963
Lockwood Addition	Helmuth, Obata & Kassabaum	1977
Thurston House (168 College)		
Tonks House (69 Raymond)	Oliver S. Tonks	1912
Town Houses	Hutchings & Moore	1971
Van Ingen Hall	Allen, Collens & Willis	1937
Van Vliet House (5 Orchard Lane)	P. T. MacLagan	1907
Van Vliet Garage	Vassar College	1921
Vassar Brothers Laboratory	Benjamin Silliman, Jr.	1880
Addition		1892
Razed		1938
Vlackte House (14 Orchard Lane)		c.1860
Addition	Vassar College	1925
Garage		1926
Walker Field House	Daniel F. Tully Assoc.	1982
Water Meter House		1926
Watson Apartments	Carl Koch & Assoc.	1966
Weaver House or Farm (Reconstructed from barn)		1917
Williams House	Hunt & Hunt	1924
Wimpfheimer Nursery School	Allen & Collens	1927
Wood House (79 Raymond)	Pilcher & Tachau	1904

Notes

[1] Cited by Rosalie Thorne McKenna, "A Study of the Architecture of the Main Building and the Landscaping of Vassar College" (Master's Thesis, Vassar College, 1949), p. 49.

[2] Benson Lossing, *Vassar College and Its Founder* (New York: Alvord, 1867), p. 149. This passage relies heavily on Lossing's first-hand account of the design and building of the Observatory, which benefitted from his interviews with Mitchell and Farrar and from his use of Farrar's diagrams.

[3] Katharine Anthony, *Louisa May Alcott* (New York: Alfred Knopf, 1938), pp. 204-06.

[4] James Monroe Taylor, "History of the Vassar Campus," *Vassar Quarterly*, I, 3, (July 1916), p. 164.

[5] Joseph Herenden Clark, *Autobiography of an Architect* (Portola Valley, California: By the Author, 1974), p. 57.

[6] Elizabeth Hazelton Haight, "Taylor Hall: The New Art Building at Vassar College," *Art and Archeology*, 2, 2 (Sept. 1915), pp. 54-55.

Books, Articles, and Other Sources

Charles Collens, "Vassar College," *Architectural Review*, 123,2411. (Jan. 17, 1923), pp. 47-55.

Edward R. Linner, *Vassar: The Remarkable Growth of a Man and His College*, Elizabeth A. Daniels, ed. (Poughkeepsie, N.Y., 1984).

Dio Lewis, *The New Gymnastics* (Boston: Ticknor & Fields, 1862).

Harriet Raymond Lloyd, *Life and Letters of John Howard Raymond* (New York: Fords, Howard and Hulbert, 1881).

Benson J. Lossing, *Historical Sketch of Vassar College* (New York: S. W. Green, 1876). *Vassar College and Its Founder* (New York: C. A. Alvord, 1867).

Henry Noble MacCracken, *The Hickory Limb* (New York: Charles Scribner's Sons, 1950).

Dorothy A. Plum and George B. Dowell, *The Great Experiment, A Chronicle of Vassar* (Poughkeepsie, N.Y., 1961).

Frances W. Swan, et al, eds., *Communications to the Board of Trustees of Vassar College by Its Founder* (New York, 1886).

Cards recording building changes, Facilities Planning office, Vassar College.
Letters, New England alumnae to Board of Trustees, 1884, Special Collections.
Maps and blueprints, various places, Vassar campus.
Miscellany News, Vassar College.
Vassarion, Vassar College.
Vassar Quarterly, Vassar College.
Vassar Views, Vassar College.